SpringerBriefs in Educational Communications and Technology

Series Editors:
J. Michael Spector, Denton, TX, USA
M.J. Bishop, Bethlehem, PA, USA
Dirk Ifenthaler, Melbourne, VIC, A'

For further volumes:
http://www.springer.com/series/11821

M. Aaron Bond • Barbara B. Lockee

Building Virtual Communities of Practice for Distance Educators

 Springer

M. Aaron Bond
Faculty Development
  and Support Services
Virginia Tech
Blacksburg, VA, USA

Barbara B. Lockee
School of Education
Virginia Tech
Blacksburg, VA, USA

ISSN 2196-498X
ISBN 978-3-319-03625-0
DOI 10.1007/978-3-319-03626-7

ISSN 2196-4998 (electronic)
ISBN 978-3-319-03626-7 (eBook)

Springer Cham Heidelberg New York Dordrecht London

Library of Congress Control Number: 2014938017

Springer is part of Springer Science+Business Media (www.springer.com)

Contents

About the Authors

Dr. M. Aaron Bond currently serves as the Director for Learning Design and Development for Networked Learning Design and Strategies (NLDS) at Virginia Tech. He has worked in the field of instructional technology, distance education, and professional development for more than 15 years. He has an earned A.A.S. from Virginia Western Community College in Education, a B.A. in History from Mary Baldwin College, an M.A. Interdisciplinary Studies from Fort Hayes State University, an Ed.S. Educational Leadership and Policy Studies from the University of Virginia, and a Ph.D. from Virginia Tech in Curriculum and Instruction. Dr. Bond has served as a corporate trainer, face-to-face classroom instructor, an online instructor, and a secondary principal.

Dr. Barbara B. Lockee is a Professor of Instructional Design and Technology and Associate Director of Educational Research and Outreach in the School of Education at Virginia Tech. She teaches courses in instructional design, message design, and distance education. Her research interests focus on instructional design issues related to technology-mediated learning. She has published more than 80 papers in academic journals, conferences, and books and has presented her scholarly work at over 100 national and international conferences. Dr. Lockee is Past President of the Association for Educational Communications and Technology, an international professional organization for educational technology researchers and practitioners. She earned her Ph.D. in 1996 from Virginia Tech in Curriculum and Instruction (Instructional Technology), M.A. in 1991 from Appalachian State University in Curriculum and Instruction (Educational Media), and B.A. in 1986 from Appalachian State University in Communication Arts.

Chapter 1
Introduction

Keywords ADDIE • Community of practice • Domain • Community • Practice • Reification • Virtual community of practice • Faculty development • Professional development • Online learning • Online teaching

As colleges, universities, and other learning institutions explore teaching and learning through online environments, online communities of practice may provide solutions to organizational and professional development needs. Guidelines for building an online community of practice based on an extensive literature review may inform higher education organizational and professional development practices. Developing a framework for online teaching and learning may help administrators evaluate faculty training needs, provide an additional resource for faculty support and development, and inform how online communities are formed and maintained (Bonk & Dennen, 2003). The purpose of this handbook is to develop a set of guidelines for creating a virtual community of practice for faculty teaching at a distance that can easily be implemented by faculty development professionals.

A community of practice (CoP), as described by cognitive anthropologists Jean Lave and Etienne Wenger, consists of a group of people who share an interest, a craft, and/or a profession (Lave & Wenger, 1991; Wenger, 1998). Communities of practice are evident in everyday situations including family units, social organizations, academia, and the workplace. Communities of practice do not exist in vacuum. Instead they exist alongside of and within other communities of practice (Wenger, 1998). A CoP exists to foster the growth of the practice through the initiation and support of those entering the practice by those considered 'masters' of the practice in a process that is founded upon mutual respect and the desire to contribute to the practice (Lave & Wenger, 1991). The community of practice shares not only a common interest and passion; it also consists of and creates its own knowledge and resources. It is only through shared experience that learners come to understand common language, slogans, and various artifacts of the culture of a particular situation (Henning, 2004). Communities of practice must consist of both participation (conversations, activities, reflections) and reification (artifacts, documents, processes, methods) for meaning making to occur (Wenger, 2010). The community of practice contributes to and expands both knowledge and resources.

Designing a virtual community of practice can be operationalized using the ADDIE model to guide the process. Based on an instructional systems design process, the ADDIE model emphasizes the five core elements of the instructional systems design process: analyze, design, develop, implement, and evaluate (Richey, Klein, & Tracey, 2011). Often the ADDIE model serves as a project management tool or to provide a visual aid for the organization of relevant tasks. Though the elements of the design process are used routinely for instructional design, they are general enough to be applicable in overall program design as well (Richey et al., 2011). The guidelines will employ the common instructional design tasks, using ADDIE—as identified by Richey et al. (2011) and Ni and Branch (2010)—as the model for operationalizing the tasks necessary for building and maintaining a virtual community of practice.

The guidelines are based on the theoretical components for building a community of practice in electronic environments. Wenger, McDermott, and Snyder (2002) identified three key elements that foster a well-rounded community: domain, community, and practice. *Domain* refers to the shared repertoire of the community, *community* addresses the interaction and role definition of members, and *practice* is the knowledge building and sharing efforts required for a community of practice to thrive. Sherer, Shea, and Kristensen (2003) expanded the Wenger et al. model by further defining each element:

- The domain: A community of practice is not just a group of friends. Involvement in the community requires some knowledge and some competence in the focus area, or domain.
- The community: Members of the community interact and learn together, they engage in joint activities and discussions, help each other, and share information.
- The practice: Members of the community develop a shared repertoire of resources: experiences, stories, tools, ways of addressing recurring problems—in short, a shared practice (Sherer et al., 2003).

Within each element there are significant tasks that can be operationalized within an ADDIE model framework. The guidelines consist of a description of those significant tasks and are operationalized according to each phase of the ADDIE model. As with most instructional design projects, the guidelines are presented in a categorical fashion and the tasks are not meant to be linear (Gustafson & Branch, 2002). Each fundamental element of a community of practice requires a distinct approach, but all three elements must be developed in parallel (Wenger et al., 2002). For example, many of the tasks require coordination with other tasks and should not be considered as entirely discreet undertakings.

The elements identified as critical features of a community of practice, noted in Table 1.1, are the result of a developmental research initiative (Richey & Klein, 2007) focused on addressing the need to establish an actual CoP within a university context.

Table 1.1 Operationalization of tasks for community of practice development by design phase and fundamental element

Phase	Common instructional design tasks (Ni & Branch, 2010; Richey et al., 2011)	Domain	Community	Practice
Analysis	Needs Assessment Problem/Solution Identification Resource Identification Learner Identification Goal/Objective Analysis	Conduct a gap analysis (Franklin, 2006; Gongla & Rizzuto, 2001). Determine primary intent of the community (Verburg & Andriessen, 2006; Wenger et al., 2002). Define the scope of the domain (Wenger et al., 2002). Assess organization alignment and seek organization support (Ardichvili, Page, & Wentling, 2002; Gongla & Rizzuto, 2001; Probst & Borzillo, 2008; Wenger et al., 2002).	Identify potential leaders, facilitators (Ardichvili et al., 2002; Probst & Borzillo, 2008; Wenger et al., 2002). Identify and assess needs of potential members (Wenger et al., 2002).	Identify common knowledge sharing infrastructure needs (McDermott, 2001; Wenger et al., 2002). Create community design (Wenger et al., 2002).
Design	Goal/Objective Formulation Sequencing of Goals Assessment/Evaluation Planning Formulation of Instructional/Non-instructional Strategies Media/Tool Selection	Create clear and strategic objectives and divide them into subtopics to promote clarity (Probst & Borzillo, 2008). Design clear rules and expectations for knowledge sharing (Ardichvili et al., 2002; Wenger et al., 2002). Design evaluation plan based on established objectives and phases of community development (Alem & Kravis, 2005; Derry & DuRussel, 1999; Schwier, Campbell, & Kenny, 2007; Wenger, Trayner, & de Laat, 2011).	Form governance committee or facilitator group (Gray, 2004; Palloff & Pratt, 1999; Probst & Borzillo, 2008; Wenger et al., 2002).	Select or design virtual medium that is easy to use, provides communication channels, and knowledge sharing capabilities (Probst & Borzillo, 2008; Scardamalia & Bereiter, 1994; Sharratt & Usoro, 2003).
Develop	Author and Produce Interventions Generate Resources Validate Materials	Create plan to mitigate disorders that may affect the development and continuation of the community of practice (Gongla & Rizzuto, 2004; Lindkvist, 2005; McLoughlin, 2001; Probst & Borzillo, 2008; Wenger et al., 2002). Develop plan for incentives or rewards for member participation (Sharratt & Usoro, 2003; Wasko & Faraj, 2005). Market community of practice to potential members (Probst & Borzillo, 2008; Wenger et al., 2002).	Train core membership/leadership/facilitation group (Ardichvili et al., 2002; Gray, 2004; Probst & Borzillo, 2008; Wenger et al., 2002). Provide mechanisms for new members to enter community (Borzillo, Aznar, & Schmitt, 2011; Probst & Borzillo, 2008; Wenger et al., 2002)	Plan face-to-face and electronic meetings/interactions (Ardichvili et al., 2002; Hildreth, Kimble, & Wright, 2000; Probst & Borzillo, 2008; Wenger et al., 2002).

(continued)

Table 1.1 (continued)

Phase	Common instructional design tasks (Ni & Branch, 2010; Richey et al., 2011)	Domain	Community	Practice
Implement	Development of Materials Implementing procedures Program Facilitation Prepare Environment Engage Learner	Launch the community of practice (Wenger et al., 2002). Design opportunities interaction with outside expertise (Probst & Borzillo, 2008; Wenger et al., 2002).	Promote trust within the community membership (Hildreth et al., 2000; Probst & Borzillo, 2008; Wenger et al., 2002). Mentor new members (Palloff & Pratt, 1999; Wenger et al., 2002). Facilitate discussions (Clawson & Bostrom, 1996; Fischer, 1998; Gray, 2004; Palloff & Pratt, 1999; Wenger et al., 2002). Recruit new core leadership/facilitation group members (Gongla & Rizzuto, 2001; Wenger et al., 2002).	Provide training for interaction and knowledge sharing through the virtual medium (Chih-Hsiung & McIsaac, 2002; Wenger et al., 2002). Build and organize a knowledge repository (Scardamalia & Bereiter, 1994; Wenger et al., 2002; Zhao & Bishop, 2011). Expand knowledge sharing to knowledge creation with well-defined research agenda (Waddock & Walsh, 1999; Wenger et al., 2002).
Evaluate	Evaluation Based on Objectives Formative and Summative Evaluation Software testing and revision	Evaluate the effectiveness of the community in context within the larger organization (Probst & Borzillo, 2008; Wenger et al., 2002).	Evaluate active membership through quality and quantity of member interactions and level of trust (Alem & Kravis, 2005; Wenger et al., 2011). Evaluate participant perceptions of learning and performance improvement (Verburg & Andriessen, 2006; Wenger et al., 2011).	Evaluate the effectiveness of the knowledge-sharing medium (Teo, Chan, Wei, & Zhang, 2003). Evaluate quality and quantity of knowledge sharing (Derry & DuRussel, 1999; Wenger et al., 2011).

A review of literature revealed the key components of the CoP model, as well as instructional design practices that would support the implementation of these necessary features toward the creation of a virtual community of practice.

Therefore, it appears that designing a virtual community of practice involves specific tasks that can be operationalized within a framework that juxtaposes the key elements of a well-rounded community against an instructional design framework. Table 1.1 illustrates this orthogonal relationship, summarizing the specific tasks for building a virtual community of practice associated with each design phase of the ADDIE model (rows) as they correspond within a given element of the community of practice model as described by Wenger et al. (2002) (columns).

1.1 Organization and Purpose

This book is intended as a guide or handbook for building a faculty community of practice. This set of guidelines for designing a virtual community of practice to support faculty engaged in distance learning efforts has both theoretical and practical implications. The purpose of the guidelines is to provide a research-based framework for instructional designers, faculty support professionals, and/or faculty developers to design communities of practice at their respective institutions. The book is organized according to the different phases of design as delineated by the ADDIE model, with chapters corresponding to each phase of design. Chapters are further organized into subsections addressing each of the three fundamental elements for designing a community of practice: domain, community, and practice. Though the guide is presented in a linear manner for sake of organization, the process of building a community of practice is definitely not a linear process. Instead the process is cyclical and should be undertaken with the big picture in mind. The information provided is meant only to serve as a guide, not as the definitive text on the subject. The guidelines are meant to be adapted to meet the needs of the faculty and support personnel engaged in community development in their respective institutions.

Chapter 2
Analysis

Abstract The analysis phase is an important piece of the larger design puzzle. A recent study of instructional designers found that the analysis phase was rated as a high operational priority, both in terms of the frequency and diversity of comments (Ozdilek and Robeck, World Conference on Educational Sciences, Nicosia, North Cyprus, 4–7 February 2009, New Trends and Issues in Educational Sciences 1(1):2046–2050, 2009). In the analysis phase it is important to analyze the situation to determine if a problem exists and to explore possible solutions to those problems. An entire project can be undermined without proper attention to detail in the analysis phase. Common tasks undertaken in during the analysis phase include conducting a gap or needs analysis, identifying stakeholders, and defining the scope of the project (Morrison et al., Designing effective instruction, John Wiley & Sons, Hoboken, NJ, 2010; Richey et al., The instructional design knowledge base: Theory, research, and practice, Routledge, New York, NY, 2011). Investing time and effort in the analysis phase can help determine whether a community of practice for faculty teaching at a distance will help solve specific problems that individual institutions, departments, or faculty face. This chapter will explore mapping common analysis phase tasks with critical activities for developing a community of practice.

Keywords ADDIE • Analysis • Gap analysis • Needs analysis • Project scope • Community of practice • Virtual community of practice • Faculty development • Professional development • Domain • Community • Practice

M.A. Bond and B.B. Lockee, *Building Virtual Communities of Practice for Distance Educators*, SpringerBriefs in Educational Communications and Technology, DOI 10.1007/978-3-319-03626-7_2, © Springer International Publishing Switzerland 2014

2.1 Fundamental Element: Domain (Table 2.1)

2.1.1 Gap Analysis

Gap analysis is the process of determining the current state and identifying where you want to be (Franklin, 2006). In other words it is the definition of the problem. As with any instructional design project, a gap analysis can help ensure that the appropriate solutions or interventions are employed and can help mitigate future problems before they arise. A thorough gap analysis can help determine whether a community of practice for faculty teaching at a distance fits within the organization's goals, management, value system, and infrastructure (Gongla & Rizzuto, 2001).

When performing a gap analysis for a virtual community of practice for faculty teaching at a distance, it is important to determine if a problem exists that can be solved with a community of practice. Franklin (2006) noted that when performing a gap analysis employee performance is the foundation upon which the success of an organization rests. Based on that model, it may be prudent to conduct a gap analysis that considers larger organizational goals and any performance (teaching and learning) gaps that faculty may have. Questions that can help conduct a gap analysis might include:

- Are there institutional gaps (online enrollments, student satisfaction, attrition rates) in which there are gaps between the current status and where the institution would like to be?
- What does the desired state look like? (more online enrollments, more faculty teaching online, greater faculty satisfaction with support opportunities, etc.)
- Are there professional development related gaps between faculty who teach on campus courses and those who teach online courses?
- Do faculty report isolation or problems managing online course loads?

Table 2.1 Operationalization of domain-related tasks during the analysis phase

Task	Faculty development operationalized example
Perform a gap analysis (Franklin, 2006; Gongla & Rizzuto, 2001).	Conduct gap analysis to determine type of community, the scope of the community, and whether a community of practice for faculty teaching at a distance aligns with organizational goals and meet faculty needs.
Identify primary intent of the community (Verburg & Andriessen, 2006; Wenger et al., 2002).	Determine whether the primary intent of the distance learning faculty community will be problem solving, best practice development, tool creation, innovation, or a combination.
Define the scope of the domain (Wenger et al., 2002).	Limit scope to distance teaching and learning topics that are central to the faculty community's identity.
Determine organization alignment and seek organizational support through assessment (Ardichvili et al., 2002; Probst & Borzillo, 2008; Wenger et al., 2002).	Build a case for a community of practice and secure organizational support.

From the gap analysis it is possible to better understand institutional and faculty needs. It is possible to determine whether a virtual community of practice is necessary and what specific support needs that the community of practice can address. Conducting a gap analysis can also help determine whether a community of practice model for professional development is the best intervention for faculty and organizational needs. The gap analysis will help determine the type/intent of the community, the scope of the community, and whether a community of practice aligns with institutional goals.

2.1.2 Determination of Community Intent

Communities of practice take many forms. Determining the intent of the community of practice in the early planning stages can help alleviate any later misunderstandings about its goals (Wenger, McDermott, & Snyder, 2002). The American Productivity and Quality Center (2001) identified four different intentions for the formation of communities of practice for professionals: (a) problem solving for everyday discipline-related issues, (b) best practice development and sharing, (c) tool and job aid creation, and (d) innovation. Given that communities of practice must have interaction and reification in order to be effective (Wenger, 1998), it is likely that a faculty community of practice would have elements of all the intentions listed above. As faculty explore teaching best practices together there is an opportunity for them to share knowledge, solve instructional problems, create shared resources, and add to the field through innovative practices and research. Though there may be a variety of intentions for a community of practice, it is important to determine a primary intent, adapt structures, roles, and activities, and then fit other activities into those structures (Wenger et al., 2002). Likewise, Verburg and Andriessen (2006) identified five typical forms of communities of practice found in the workplace or professional organizations: (a) daily practice community—workers or participants who meet regularly to share and create knowledge, generally face-to-face; (b) formal expert community—a limited number of experts who influence knowledge for a larger community; (c) informal network community—an open membership group that forms through common interests, generally administered through electronic means; (d) problem solving community—geographically and organizationally dispersed members who deal with the same issues or problems, or an advisory group that is formed to solve a solitary problem; and (e) latent network community—members of a professional organization like the Association for Educational Communications and Technology (AECT). A community of practice that is designed to meet the professional development needs of faculty teaching at a distance may meet the definition of a problem-solving community as described by Verburg and Andriessen, but could easily fit one of the other forms. Table 2.2 offers examples of how faculty communities of practice might be defined within each community of practice type. Determining the intent of the community will help with other areas of the design process.

Table 2.2 Faculty community of practice example by community of practice type

Community of practice type (Verburg & Andriessen, 2006)	Faculty community of practice example
Daily Practice	*Departmental community.* Faculty from the same department or unit share teaching practices specific to subject matter or organizational knowledge specific to the department.
Formal Expert	*Expert community.* Small group of faculty and administrators from across disciplines—who are known experts in a specific area—exchange or develop a strategic knowledge for influencing the institution's policies and practices. The formal expert community may prove to be core leadership group for other communities of practice.
Informal Network	*Interest community.* Faculty community formed to explore a specific topic of interest. Interest communities can form and dissolve very quickly based on hot topics of research.
Problem-Solving	*Practice community.* Faculty from different disciplines meet regularly to improve teaching practices, share resources and ideas, or solve pedagogical problems. Community participants can create and organize an institutional knowledge base or influence larger fields of study.
Latent Network	*Network community.* Faculty or industry representatives with high degrees of knowledge interact through conference or government organizations. Participation is often low or peripheral by most members.

2.1.3   Defining the Scope

Defining the scope of a design project can create parameters with appropriate boundaries, prepare allocation of resources, and set the stage for goal or objective setting in later planning stages (Morrison, Ross, Kemp, & Kalman, 2010; Richey, Klein, & Tracey, 2011). Since the scope of a community of practice for faculty teaching at a distance may vary widely, it is important to define the scope by limiting the community of practice knowledge-sharing ideas to specific topics. Wenger et al. (2002) suggested that the scope be wide enough to bring in new people, but still narrow enough to keep members interested in the community. Faculty teaching at a distance may have interests or needs that span the normal spectrum of faculty life, including tenure, work/life conflict, and other university commitments (Schroeder, 2011). Though it is tempting to try to address every interest or need that faculty may have in a single community of practice, the focus of a community of practice for online teaching and learning will have greater success if the scope defines parameters that limit potential topics to online teaching pedagogy and technology. Defining the focus and purpose of a community of practice early in the design process will provide an identity that will carry through all other design tasks (Wenger et al., 2002).

2.1.4 Assess Organizational Alignment and Secure Support

Smith and Ragan (2005) insisted that instructional system design must include an analysis of organization philosophies and restrictions. In order to be successful, communities of practice must have the support of the organization within which they exist. Communities of practice must align with the objectives of the organization in order to secure buy in from the larger organization leadership and the community members (Wenger et al., 2002). If there is no support from the larger college, department, or university for improving distance teaching and learning practices, faculty will be less motivated to participate. Additionally, without strong institutional or organizational support, communities of practice tend to fade away (Ardichvili, Page, & Wentling, 2002).

Since communities of practice that exist without the support of organization leaders rarely last, securing buy-in from the organizational leadership is imperative (Gongla & Rizzuto, 2004). University administrators and other managers are more likely to offer support for a community of practice if presented with a well-researched proposal (Wenger et al., 2002). Building a case for a community of practice can help with other tasks described so far, such as narrowing the focus and intent of the community of practice. Wenger et al. (2002) suggested that a proposal for building a community of practice should contain: an introduction to the potential value of the community of practice to the organization and rationale for support, a description of time-saving benefits of knowledge sharing ("not reinventing the wheel"), and a demonstration of how a community of practice can improve practices and prepare members to be thought leaders in the field. Probst and Borzillo (2008) found that an unhealthy competition for resources caused many communities of practice to fail even though they had organizational support. Therefore, it might be prudent to extend the proposal to include a request for resources and include a means for administrative participation in the community itself. Depending on the findings of the gap analysis, a proposal to secure buy in for a community of practice for faculty teaching at a distance may stress a community of practice as a means for faculty to improve morale, to share teaching practices, and to add to the research in the field of distance learning and/or instructional practices in a specific discipline. The addition of a list of possible ways that a university can provide support to the community of practice might include professional development resources such as conference registration and travel funding, or acquisition of software or tools needed to participate in community events or try out new teaching tools. Securing support early will clarify the community of practice domain and help mitigate problems that may arise as the community is formed (Wenger et al., 2002).

2.2   Fundamental Element: Community (Table 2.3)

2.2.1   Identify and Recruit Core Group

Designing a community of practice requires a strong core group dedicated to the creation of the community. Wenger et al. (2002) insisted that the most important component of a community's success is the vitality of its membership. During the earliest stages, the community of practice relies heavily on the core leadership to recruit members, set goals, plan activities, build trust, and establish norms, roles and scope of the community of practice (Gongla & Rizzuto, 2001; Tarmizi & de Vreede, 2005; Wenger et. al., 2002). Community of practice development often begins with an established social network. Those who are already participating in an informal group are more likely to form the core group of a community of practice and take the lead in its construction (Wenger et al., 2002).

Identifying faculty teaching at a distance who already share practices and resources is an important first step in forming the core facilitation or leadership group. Additionally, faculty support personnel should be actively recruited as they may have access to the most current teaching and learning research and can help identify faculty teaching at a distance who might benefit from participation in a community of practice (Heath & McDonald, 2012). To legitimize the community of practice, it is important to identify and recruit potential cutting-edge *thought leaders* in the field who are well-seasoned practitioners (Wenger et al., 2002) and are vocally passionate about the community topic (Gray, 2004). Core membership for a community of practice for distance faculty should comprise individuals who are excited about distance teaching and learning and who exhibit best practices in their courses.

Once potential members of the core group have been identified, a plan for recruitment can be devised. It is important to understand why potential leaders would want to participate in a community of practice. Faculty are motivated by a variety of intrinsic and external factors. While Kiziltepe (2008) found enthusiastic students, social status, and prestige from research publications were factors influencing faculty motivation, Meyer and Evans (2003) found peer recognition, opportunity to advance in their field, study leave, access to resources, and conference attendance to be among the highest ranked. Based on those motivational factors, participation in the core leadership group of a community of practice for distance faculty may fit

Table 2.3 Operationalization of community related tasks during the analysis phase

Task	Faculty development operationalized example
Identify and recruit potential leaders, facilitators (Ardichvili et al., 2002; Gongla & Rizzuto, 2001; Gray, 2004; Heath & McDonald, 2012; Kiziltepe, 2008; Meyer & Evans, 2003; Probst & Borzillo, 2008; Wenger et al., 2002).	Identify faculty support personnel and faculty teaching at a distance to serve as potential members of the core leadership group and then actively recruit the core group membership using motivational factors for faculty to encourage participation.
Identify and assess potential members needs (Wenger et al., 2002).	Identify faculty who teach at a distance and conduct interviews to assess potential member needs.

well with the professional needs of potential leaders. Recruitment activities should include a description of how potential leaders can find research opportunities, peer recognition, and incorporate best teaching practices that enhance student enthusiasm through participation. If institutional support includes financial incentives, then faculty recruitment may include support for conference attendance and study leave. Participation benefits including research opportunities, study leave, and conference attendance should be included in recruitment strategies. Like anything else that requires a commitment of time/energy/money—the benefits need to be very clear to the participants.

2.2.2 Identify and Assess Potential Members' Needs

It is important to have a good understanding of the potential members that the community of practice may serve. As has been discovered, communities of practice usually build on preexisting personal networks (Wenger et al., 2002). Since communities of practice have varying levels of participation, it is valuable to identify faculty teaching at a distance who are currently engaged in ongoing conversations around teaching and learning, as well as those not engaged in those activities. Although they may not participate, all faculty teaching at a distance are potential members of a community of practice.

Once potential members have been identified, a thorough gap analysis can help determine whether a community of practice for faculty teaching at a distance fits the professional development needs of the potential members (Wenger et al., 2002). As mentioned in the last section, faculty are motivated by a variety of factors. Finding ways to match potential benefits with faculty needs is an important step when developing a community of practice. Wenger et al. (2002) suggested that members of the core leadership group or a community coordinator should interview potential members in order to better understand common issues and needs shared by potential community members. Having an open dialogue rather than a formal interview may uncover an array of issues or topics that may not fit well within a community of practice model or change the focus and intent of the community of practice design. If a community of practice does seem to fit the potential member needs it is important to express how a community of practice may help meet the identified needs. Table 2.4 provides examples of how, in the analysis phase, community-related tasks may be operationalized for a faculty community of practice.

Table 2.4 Operationalization of practice related tasks during the analysis phase

Task	Faculty development operationalized example
Identify common knowledge sharing infrastructure needs (McDermott, 2001; Wenger et al., 2002).	Assess infrastructure needs for sharing knowledge through interviews with potential members and core leadership group membership.
Create community design (Wenger et al., 2002).	Create a comprehensive community design plan using the Analysis Phase Sample Community Design Planning Document (see Appendix A).

2.3 Fundamental Element: Practice

2.3.1 Identify Common Knowledge-Sharing Infrastructure Needs

A significant part of developing an understanding of potential community members in the analysis phase is the determination of the knowledge needs of potential members. Though communities of practice frequently form around topics community members have invested many years in developing, communities of practice are not formed just around a common interest. Communities of practice focus on practice, problems, tools, developments in the field, and things that work and things that do not work (McDermott, 2001). As discussed in the last section, conducting a gap analysis is a critical part of the analysis stage. When interviewing potential members to discover issues and needs, it is important to determine knowledge-sharing needs for the virtual community of practice. There are many potential knowledge-sharing needs that should be addressed. Wenger et al. (2002) identified the seven online technology infrastructure considerations that are critical for knowledge sharing: (a) a home page, (b) a conversation space for online discussions, (c) a repository for documents, research reports, best practices, and standards, (d) a search engine to find resources in the knowledge base, (e) a directory of membership, (f) a shared workspace for collaboration, and (g) community management tools including page counters, participation tracking, and the like. There are a number of tools that can meet the infrastructure considerations described above. When designing a virtual community of practice for faculty, the selection of a particular tool should be based on the specific needs as identified by a gap analysis.

2.3.2 Create Community Design

As with any design project, conducting a needs assessment and planning are key. It is in the analysis phase when it becomes clear whether the issue or problem has a possible design solution (Richey et al., 2011). During the analysis stage it is important to develop a clear plan for the community of practice that includes multiple opportunities for assessing needs of potential members, organizational needs, and the infrastructural or framework needs for a community of practice to develop. Wenger et al. (2002) suggested employing a work plan in the early planning stages to define the community's focus, build relationships, and identify topics and projects.

Using a checklist or a planning document may help ensure that all essential tasks are considered. Once the planning document has been completed designers can move the plan into action in later phases of the design process. It is important to note that the planning document can be used to determine whether a community of practice for faculty teaching at a distance is the appropriate solution for the audience, issues, or problem that one is seeking to address. It is possible that a community of practice model will not meet a given institution, potential membership, or programmatic need. Appropriate planning and assessment in the analysis phase may deter potential problems in later phases (Smith & Ragan, 2005). Appendix A provides an example of a community design document that incorporates all components and tasks for a faculty community of practice during the analysis phase.

Chapter 3
Design

Abstract Robert Mager (Preparing instructional objectives: A critical tool in the development of effective instruction, CEP Press, Atlanta, GA, 1997) famously says in reference to instructional objectives, "If you're not sure where you're going, you're liable to end up some place else" (p. vi). It is in the design phase that the road map for a project is created. Common tasks in the design phase include the formation of objectives, formation of evaluation materials, and media selection. Without clearly stated goals and objectives a project might easily veer off track. This is especially true for the development of a community of practice for professional development purposes. In this chapter we will explore the creation of a road map by discussing the formation of organizational objectives and instructional objectives, the creation of evaluation materials that assess stated objectives, and the selection of tools that may effectively facilitate a virtual community of practice.

Keywords ADDIE • Design • Organizational objectives • Instructional objectives • Evaluation plan • Community of practice • Virtual community of practice • Faculty development • Professional development • Domain • Community • Practice • Knowledge-sharing • Media selection

3.1 Fundamental Element: Domain (Table 3.1)

3.1.1 Goal/Objective Creation and Categorization

Formation of goals and objectives help guide the design and development process. Also called outcomes, objectives "serve as a road map—an instructional mission statement of where you're headed and what you are trying to achieve" (Cennamo & Kalk, 2005, p. 51). When researching common factors impacting the viability of communities of practice in 57 separate organizations, Probst and Borzillo (2008) found that the formation of strategic goals, divided into subtopics for clarification

M.A. Bond and B.B. Lockee, *Building Virtual Communities of Practice for Distance Educators*, SpringerBriefs in Educational Communications and Technology, DOI 10.1007/978-3-319-03626-7_3, © Springer International Publishing Switzerland 2014

Table 3.1 Operationalization of domain related tasks during the design phase

Task	Faculty development operationalized example
Create clear and strategic objectives and divide them into subtopics to promote clarity (Probst & Borzillo, 2008).	Form objectives for a virtual community of practice for faculty professional development that describe and encourage knowledge sharing, improved practices, and reification.
Design clear rules and expectations for knowledge sharing (Ardichvili et al., 2002; Wenger et al., 2002).	Create rules and expectations with the core membership that address faculty concerns including state and federal regulations, institutional policies or norms, and intellectual property.
Design evaluation plan based on established objectives and phases of community development (Alem & Kravis, 2005; Derry & DuRussel, 1999; Schwier, Campbell, & Kenny, 2007; Wenger et al., 2011).	Create a plan using broad questions with the intention of guiding later evaluations. Align evaluation questions with established objectives to determine whether the community of practice is meeting established objectives and desired outcomes.

for all stakeholders, is critical for communities of practice to grow and thrive. The authors also suggested that, when objectives provide clear and measurable goals, community of practice participants are more likely to actively participate in the process of best practice development and sharing because potential benefits and outcomes are clearly defined. Additionally, organizational leaders are more likely to provide support for a community of practice when goals and outcomes are clearly delineated (Probst & Borzillo, 2008; Wenger, McDermott, & Snyder, 2002) [and tied to the institutional mission/goals/strategic plan]. Objectives that define the areas of focus, describe expected outcomes, and outline participant responsibilities can provide the *road map* for moving a community of practice forward.

Objectives or outcomes for a virtual community of practice for online teaching faculty should address institutional and participant needs, encourage improved instructional practices, and define how the community will move to reification. Objectives will vary depending on the specific goals and needs of a particular institution or group of faculty. Table 3.2 offers examples of possible objectives.

3.1.2 Knowledge Sharing Rule and Expectation Design

Knowledge sharing is a key element of a community of practice. The formation of expectations about how to participate and share knowledge in appropriate ways is necessary for promoting trust and a healthy community of practice. Such expectations are not meant to serve as punitive measures. Though groups may form sporadically around a topic about which participants are passionate, passion is not enough to effectively form and coalesce a community of practice. over a period of time Potential participants in a community of practice must be willing to engage in collaboration with a negotiated activity, must see the community as a joint

Table 3.2 Sample objectives by fundamental element

Fundamental element	Examples
Domain	The virtual community of practice for online teaching faculty will define how institutional support is in alignment with university or departmental strategic plan.
	The virtual community of practice for online teaching faculty will support institutional goals.
Community	Members of the virtual community of practice for online teaching faculty will demonstrate online teaching and learning best practices.
	Members of the virtual community of practice for online teaching faculty will participate in knowledge sharing.
	Members of the virtual community of practice for online teaching faculty will assist one another to improve instructional practices across the institution or department.
Practice	Members of the virtual community of practice for online teaching faculty will add to the field of online teaching and learning by researching instructional practices in their courses.
	Members of the virtual community of practice for online teaching faculty will add to the field of online teaching and learning by disseminating research findings at conferences or through publications.

enterprise that demands ownership and accountability, and must view meaning making in the community as a shared repertoire (Wenger, 1998). Communities of practice must consist of both participation (conversations, activities, reflections) and reification (artifacts, documents, processes, methods) for meaning making to occur (Wenger, 2010). When conducting a study of virtual communities of practice in several different organizations, Ardichvili, Page, and Wentling (2002) found that without clearly communicated standards for what constitutes knowledge sharing and what specific information violates security policy or other rules, participants were less likely to engage in knowledge sharing.

Participants in a faculty community of practice may have anxieties about the nature and security of any knowledge that is shared with the community. Faculty may be concerned about how sharing instructional practices is effected by institutional policies or federal or state regulations such as FERPA. Additionally, faculty may have reservations about preserving their intellectual property (Meyer & Evans, 2003). When constructing rules and expectations for knowledge sharing and reification within the community of practice, the core leadership team must address the institutional policies, FERPA regulations, and how to protect faculty intellectual property.

3.1.3 Evaluation Plan Creation

Evaluation is a key element of the design process. There are many possible avenues for evaluating the effectiveness of a community of practice. Communities of practice can be evaluated to determine the effectiveness of the community of practice in

Table 3.3 Evaluation questions alignment with sample objectives

Sample objectives	Evaluation question
The virtual community of practice for online teaching faculty will define how institutional support is in alignment with university or departmental strategic plan.	Describe how the virtual community of practice defines its role within the larger university or departmental strategic plan?
The virtual community of practice for online teaching faculty will support institutional goals.	Provide examples of how the virtual community of practice supports institutional goals?
Members of the virtual community of practice for online teaching faculty will demonstrate online teaching and learning best practices.	How are members of the virtual community of practice demonstrating best practices in their online courses?
Members of the virtual community of practice for online teaching faculty will participate in knowledge sharing.	Explain how members of the community participate in knowledge sharing?
Members of the virtual community of practice for online teaching faculty will assist one another to improve instructional practices across the institution or department.	Do members assist one another across departments or the institution to improve instructional practices?
Members of the virtual community of practice for online teaching faculty will add to the field of online teaching and learning by researching instructional practices in their courses.	How are members contributing to the field of online teaching and learning by researching their instructional practices?
Members of the virtual community of practice for online teaching faculty will add to the field of online teaching and learning by disseminating research findings at conferences or through publications.	Are members disseminating findings at conferences or through publications?

context of the larger organization (Verburg & Andriessen, 2006; Wenger et al., 2002), by the quality and quantity of member interactions and level of trust (Alem & Kravis, 2005; Wenger, Trayner, & de Laat, 2011), from participant perceptions of learning and performance improvement (Wenger et al., 2011), by quality and quantity of knowledge sharing (Derry & DuRussel, 1999; Wenger et al., 2011), and the overall performance of the knowledge sharing media (Teo, Chan, Wei, & Zhang, 2003). The areas of focus for evaluation will be discussed at length in the evaluation phase section. In this section alignment of evaluations will be the focus. Evaluation can occur at any time during the design phase (Richey, Klein, & Tracey, 2011). To ensure that an evaluation incorporates effective measures, the evaluation plan should be formulated when goals and objectives are initially created (Ni & Branch, 2010; Smith & Ragan, 2005; Wenger et al., 2011). Creating an evaluation plan at this stage with overarching questions can help determine later whether outcomes are being met by the community of practice (Smith & Ragan, 2005; Wenger et al., 2002). Additionally, creating an evaluation plan can help "right the course" if the community of practice is stalling, veering away from established objectives, or being disrupted. In previous sections, objectives were discussed and example objectives for a faculty community of practice were defined. Using those objectives as an example, Table 3.3 offers examples of how evaluation planning at this stage of the process can help to ensure alignment.

3.2   Fundamental Element: Community (Table 3.4)

3.2.1   Formation of a Core Group

The most important factor impacting the viability of a community of practice is the core group membership (Gray, 2004; Probst & Borzillo, 2008; Wenger et al., 2002). In the analysis phase, potential community leaders were identified and recruited. In this phase, community leaders are asked to coalesce and form a governance body. Core members will help write objectives and form the knowledge sharing expectations for the community of practice. As faculty have limited time to dedicate to extraneous activities, it is important to provide the likely time commitment for potential leaders. Spreading leadership responsibilities among several key community members can help with time demands. If possible, dedicating a faculty support position or portion of a support position to organizing community events can help further spread the community's organizational duties (Heath & McDonald, 2012). Having faculty and support personnel serve as members of the core group may help with the viability of the larger community of practice. Several informal events should be planned to allow the core group to define the community's goals, expectations, and rules. Informal meetings and discussions can allow the group to form relationships, and build trust (Wenger et al., 2002).

3.3   Fundamental Element: Practice (Table 3.5)

3.3.1   Media Selection

Finding a platform for hosting a virtual community of practice is critical to building and maintaining a community of practice (Hemp, 2009). Any virtual platform for a community of practice will likely serve as a repository that allows all participants access to the community's co-constructed knowledge and provides a forum for storytelling (Probst & Borzillo, 2008). Scardamalia and Bereiter (1994) found that technology must provide the infrastructure for collaboration instead of being the catalyst. Opportunities for interaction must be designed to support knowledge-building communities by: (a) providing a community database at the center of discourse, (b) emphasizing writing and intentionality as mechanisms for discourse, (c) leveraging a distributed model of computing, and (d) encouraging multiple modes of communication (Scardamalia & Bereiter, 1994). Though a potential virtual medium may have clear channels for communication and a shared repository, if the information systems are not easy to use or not perceived as useful by participants, the platform will hinder or be ignored by the community (Sharratt & Usoro, 2003).

Table 3.4 Operationalization of community related tasks during the design phase

Task	Faculty development operationalized example
Form governance committee or facilitator group (Gray, 2004; Heath & McDonald, 2012; Palloff & Pratt, 1999; Probst & Borzillo, 2008; Wenger et al., 2002).	Promote core group coalescence through informal meetings and discussions. Define goals, objectives, expectations, and rules for the community of practice (core group).

Table 3.5 Operationalization of practice related tasks during the design phase

Task	Faculty development operationalized example
Select or design virtual media that is easy to use, provides communication channels, and knowledge sharing capabilities (Probst & Borzillo, 2008; Scardamalia & Bereiter, 1994; Sharratt & Usoro, 2003).	Select virtual tools considering faculty knowledge sharing needs and technical competencies. Use institution supported LMS if possible. If not, select tools that provide a safe environment for discussion and a knowledge repository. Use synchronous tools and social media with caution, understanding possible distractions or disruptions can blur professional and personal identities.

Table 3.6 Possible tools by virtual community of practice technology need

Need	Possible tool
Online Interaction/Discussion	• Institution Supported Learning Management System (Blackboard, Sakai, Desire2Learn, etc.) • LISTSERV • Forums (Piazza, LMS Discussion Board, etc.) • Blogs (Blogger, Word Press, etc.) • Web Conferencing (Centra, WebX, GoToMeeting, Adobe Connect, Collaborate, etc.) • Social Media (Facebook, Twitter, etc.)
Knowledge Creation/Sharing	• Wikis (LMS wiki, Wikispaces, etc.) • Blogs (Blogger, Word Press, etc.) • Web Conferencing • Document Collaboration Tools (Google Drive, Dropbox, etc.)
Document Repositories	• Institution Supported Learning Management System (Blackboard, Sakai, Desire2Learn, etc.) • Wikis (LMS wiki, Wikispaces, etc.) • Document Collaboration Tools (Google Drive, Dropbox, etc.)

When considering tools or platforms for hosting a virtual community of practice for faculty teaching online it is important to consider technical competencies of potential members and find tools that match faculty competencies. If possible, using the same Learning Management System (LMS) that faculty work with each day may be an effective way to address the many issues that may arise when using a tool or medium that faculty find unfamiliar. If the LMS does not meet knowledge-sharing or discussion needs of the virtual community of practice, tools selected or created should be easy to use while also providing a space that is secure, that allows for rich discussion, and that facilitates the creation of a knowledge-sharing repository (Probst & Borzillo, 2008; Scardamalia & Bereiter, 1994; Sharratt & Usoro, 2003). Other tools, such as synchronous web conferencing, chat, and social media should be undertaken with great caution as the virtual community may be disrupted when there is lack of familiarity with tools or lines of professional and personal participation are blurred (Cox, Carr, & Hall, 2004; Durkee et al., 2009; Kear, 2011). Table 3.6 provides examples of possible tools for virtual community of practice needs.

Though a potential virtual medium may have clear channels for communication and a repository, if the information systems are not easy to use or not perceived as useful by participants the platform will hinder the community (Sharratt & Usoro, 2003).

Chapter 4
Develop

Abstract The development phase the ADDIE model is the phase in which interventions are authored and produced (Richey et al., The instructional design knowledge base: Theory, research, and practice, Routledge, New York, NY, 2011). Common tasks in the development phase include designing interactions, creating instructional materials, and building required mechanisms and processes. This chapter will explore the unique development strategies for building a virtual community of practice for faculty teaching at a distance.

Keywords ADDIE • Development • Membership recruitment • Mentorship • Community of practice • Virtual community of practice • Faculty development • Professional development • Domain • Community • Practice

4.1 Fundamental Element: Domain (Table 4.1)

4.1.1 Create Plan to Mitigate Potential Disruptions

Communities of practice are not without problems. There is a constant threat of *groupthink* for any community of practice. Incorrect behaviors, ideals, and dogmas are often perpetuated through group participation due to the positive reinforcements that consensus provides (Rogers & Skinner, 1956; Skinner, 1967). Just because a group comes to a consensus does not mean that constructed meaning is the correct meaning or the most appropriate path forward (Janis, 1972; Lindkvist, 2005). It is important to safeguard the integrity of the knowledge-building process while minimizing the persistence of groupthink. Possible safeguards against groupthink for an online faculty community of practice might include exposure to external perspectives and approaches, course reviews, and submission of research to peer-reviewed conferences or publications.

Table 4.1 Operationalization of domain related tasks during the development phase

Task	Faculty development operationalized example
Create plan to mitigate disorders that may affect the development and continuation of the community of practice (Gongla & Rizzuto, 2004; Lindkvist, 2005; McLoughlin, 2001; Probst & Borzillo, 2008; Wenger et al., 2002).	Use internal and external peer review process to minimize persistence of groupthink. Identify potential threats and create plan to address potential disruptions to the community of practice (core group).
Develop plan for incentives or rewards for member participation (Sharratt & Usoro, 2003; Wasko & Faraj, 2005).	Utilize institutional support to create awards. Employ institutional dissemination methods to publish names, pictures, and contributions of faculty participants. Promote community of practice mentorships and access to resources.
Market community of practice to potential members (Probst & Borzillo, 2008; Wenger et al., 2002).	Employ institutional dissemination methods to build a case for membership. Recruit members using the benefits of contributing and the value of learning from other's experience.

The desire to provide a formal structure for collaboration can inadvertently create a culture built around deadlines, milestones, and rigid structures that hinders meaning making for the community (Lindkvist, 2005; Wenger, McDermott, & Snyder, 2002). Gongla and Rizzuto (2004) asserted that communities of practice can disappear or fade into nonexistence, especially when there is formal inquiry within the larger organization that houses the community of practice. Wenger et al. (2002) identified 13 internal disorders that may affect the development and continuation of communities of practice: (a) narcissism—the community may become self-absorbed, pursuing their own agenda without any regard to outside interests, (b) marginality—a community outside the mainstream has no decision-making power within an organization and is often made up of participants who share discontent, (c) factionalism—a community can be torn apart internally by members fighting for their own personal interests or ideas, (d) cliques—a community can stagnate by focusing on relationships among a core membership while minimizing efforts to recruit new members, (e) egalitarianism—a community can constrain creativity, viewing new ways of thinking as treasonous rather than ideas to explore (similar to groupthink), (f) dependence—a community can become reliant on the charisma or leadership of one person or small group of people, (g) stratification—a community can concentrate power or decision making in a small core group of experts, leading to lack of diversity or distinct classes of participants, (h) disconnectedness—a community's members participate superficially, there is no personal connection to the group or its central ideals, (i) localism—a community becomes defined by its geographical, departmental, or other boundaries, (j) documentism—a community's focus becomes documentation rather than knowledge sharing and construction, (k) amnesia—a community focuses on social discussions with no documentation or knowledge management, (l) dogmatism—a community's members refuse to deviate from established canons and methods, or (m) mediocrity—a community falls into a routine that accepts the status quo rather than forging new ideas or innovations.

Table 4.2 Possible interventions to mitigate problems

Threat (Wenger et al., 2002)	Intervention
Groupthink	Use internal and external peer review process to minimize persistence of groupthink.
Narcissism	Create clear goals and objectives that identify the role of community of practice in institutional context.
Marginality	Allow for discontent and gripe sessions, but use facilitation to move the conversation forward. Avoid turning the community into a community of discontent, by harnessing those who express discontent with visible responsibilities.
Factionalism	Promote debate, but avoid internal strife. Employ deliberate activities to enhance reification and highlight strategic alignment with needs of the institution.
Cliques	Plan for active recruitment and inclusion of new members to ensure that the community of practice has fresh membership.
Egalitarianism	Promote open dialogue and respect for diverse perspectives.
Dependence	Actively recruit core members, facilitators, or coordinators with leadership roles shifting at regular intervals.
Stratification	Engage entire community in problem solving or group decision-making.
Disconnectedness	Engage entire community in knowledge-sharing events and decision-making.
Localism	Create events in which the community can interact with other communities of practice, departments, or institutions.
Documentism	Define the purpose of documents, identify those that would be useful, and develop clear roles for document management. Documentation should be integrated with knowledge sharing and problem solving activities.
Amnesia	Ensure discussions and reification are recorded and organized appropriately in the virtual environment.
Dogmatism	Encourage involvement in innovative projects and development of the practice of online teaching and learning.
Mediocrity	Analyze current research in online teaching and learning. Discuss findings and ways to replicate the studies or improve on them.

Threats to a thriving community must be considered when designing and maintaining any community of practice. Table 4.2 provides possible interventions to mitigate threats to community. A community of practice for faculty teaching online may face unique challenges not yet identified. Each community of practice must rely on the core members or facilitators to identify potential threats and implement appropriate interventions (Wenger et al., 2002).

4.1.2 Form Rewards/Incentives Plan

For many teaching faculty the possibility of enhanced reputation or the altruism of helping others is incentive enough to share knowledge and best practices. The expectation of knowledge sharing can cause less participation in a virtual community.

For some experts, sharing knowledge can mean giving up a sense of power that comes from holding onto that same knowledge (Carroll et al., 2003; Gray, 2001). In this case, there must be a comparable incentive or reward for sharing knowledge. Regardless of the motivating factors affecting knowledge sharing, there must be an incentive or reward plan for encouraging continued participation. As institutions and departments face budget cuts, there is little money to spare for funding monetary rewards or incentives. For that reason the discussion here will focus on the creation of a rewards/incentives plan that does not involve monetary commitments.

Finding no-cost ways to reward participation in a community of practice can be a daunting task. There are ways to reward participation, however. Sharratt and Usoro (2003) found that when there is opportunity for recognition, such as career advancement or reputation building, members are more likely to participate in community of practice dialogue and knowledge sharing. Likewise, Wasko and Faraj (2005) found that enhanced reputation may provide reward enough for some community of practice participants. As mentioned in the analysis section, faculty are motivated by social status and prestige from research publications (Kiziltepe, 2008), peer recognition, opportunity to advance in their field, study leave, and access to resources (Meyer & Evans, 2003). If there is limited funding a plan for rewarding or incentivizing faculty who participate in the virtual community of practice must include ways to recognize and acknowledge the contributions of members. Faculty looking for career advancement may be reluctant to participate in a community of practice if the community does not have institutional support. Using institutional support to provide recognition such as a certificate of appreciation from senior level management can be an incentive for those wishing to enhance their reputation or advance in their field. Since faculty are motivated by peer recognition, one reward strategy might be to publish names and contributions on departmental, institution, and community of practice websites, newsfeeds, or other dissemination methods available across the university. Additionally, the resources and peer mentoring available through a community of practice can also serve as an incentive. Faculty participation may be motivated through a variety of means. Providing multiple avenues for rewarding and incentivizing participation is key for knowledge sharing and participation in a community of practice (Wang & Lai, 2006; Wasko & Faraj, 2005). Rather than inventing new structures, it may be possible to work within established reward and incentive structures at the institution. Table 4.3 offers possible incentives for encouraging faculty participation.

4.1.3 Market the Community to Potential Members

In order for members to join a community of practice, they must first know that it exists. It is often the community coordinators or facilitators who drive the information and recruitment efforts of a community of practice (Probst & Borzillo, 2008; Wenger et al., 2002). Recruiting potential members of a virtual community of practice for faculty teaching online requires unique marketing strategies based on faculty motivational factors as described in the analysis phase and in the previous section. Wenger et al., suggested that marketing efforts follow a two-pronged

Table 4.3 Possible incentives/rewards by motivation

Incentives/rewards	Examples
Administrative Recognition	• Certificate of Appreciation
	• Course Load Release
	• Educational Leave
	• Research Leave
Peer Recognition	• Leadership Opportunities within the Community
	• News Releases/Promotions
	• Publications, Grants, etc.
Monetary	• Leadership Stipend
	• Conference Travel
	• Outreach Opportunities
	• Technology or Other Resources

approach that highlights the benefits of contributing and the value of learning from other's experiences. By using university dissemination methods including LISTSERV services, websites, publications, or events, it is possible to describe the potential benefits of participation in a community of practice for faculty teaching online at little or no cost. This form of communication also allows placing the community of practice within the scope of the larger institution.

4.2 Fundamental Element: Community (Table 4.4)

4.2.1 Core Membership Training

As discussed previously, the core membership is often described as the most important factor for the success of a community of practice. Gray (2004) suggested that the key characteristics of a core team member are technical competence, an understanding of community or relationship building, an orientation for learning, and sufficient knowledge of the practice. Wenger et al. (2002) identified seven key functions that community coordinators perform: (a) identify important issues in the domain, (b) plan and facilitate community events, (c) link community members with assets, organizational units, and institutional leaders, (d) foster development of community members, (e) manage the boundary between the community and other organizational units, (f) help build the practice, and (g) assess the health of the community of practice and evaluate its contributions. Given the important role that core leaders play in the development of a thriving community, training and professional development of potential facilitators should be taken seriously. Training should encompass facilitation techniques, relationship building, technologies used for the community of practice, balancing authority and power, promoting trust, and encouraging participation (Ardichvili, Page, & Wentling, 2002; Fallah, 2011). As every community of practice is different, it is imperative to identify and leverage the different skill sets that a given group of leaders possess. Specific professional development will depend on the particular needs of a community of practice and the skills that a group of coordinators may have.

Table 4.4 Operationalization of community related tasks during the development phase

Task	Faculty development operationalized example
Train core membership/leadership/facilitation group (Ardichvili et al., 2002; Gray, 2004; Probst & Borzillo, 2008; Wenger et al., 2002).	Provide professional development that encompasses facilitation techniques, relationship building, and technologies used for the community of practice, how to balance authority and power, how to promote trust, and how to encourage participation and reification.
Provide mechanisms for new members to enter community (Borzillo et al., 2011; Probst & Borzillo, 2008; Wenger et al., 2002).	Display directions for joining the virtual community with contact information for core group members responsible for the technical support or further information.

4.2.2 Build Mechanisms for Onboarding New Members

As mentioned earlier when discussing threats to a thriving community, communities of practice that do not actively recruit and engage new members face stagnation or decline (Probst & Borzillo, 2008; Wenger et al., 2002). In order to encourage growth, a plan should be devised to allow new online teaching faculty members to assimilate into the community of practice. It is important to remember that not all new members will actively participate in the community of practice even though they will benefit from participating on the periphery. Potential members should have access to participation in an open and peripheral manner. Communities of practice can ease the onboarding process for new members by providing a clear set of directions for joining the community. Gaining access to a community of practice LISTSERV or the institution supported LMS should be an open process. If potential members perceive a community of practice is closed or not welcoming, they will not attempt to join (Borzillo, Aznar, & Schmitt, 2011). Core group members or facilitators should design clear directions for joining the community of practice and post them prominently on institutional, departmental, or community practice websites with contact information for further information and technical support.

4.3 Fundamental Element: Practice (Table 4.5)

4.3.1 Plan Interactions

While virtual community of practice participants may meet informally to discuss topics of interest or to work on reification projects at any time, regular meetings with the larger community are required. Wenger et al. (2002) suggested that regularly scheduled events help establish a sense of familiarity and create a rhythm for the community of practice. Whether meetings are held face to face, solely online, or

Table 4.5 Operationalization of practice related tasks during the development phase

Task	Faculty development operationalized example
Plan face-to-face and electronic meetings/ interactions (Ardichvili et al., 2002; Hildreth et al., 2000; Probst & Borzillo, 2008; Wenger et al., 2002).	Schedule a series of regularly occurring events to create a rhythm and a sense of familiarity. Follow-up with email invitations and/or alerts to prospective members. Provide schedule of upcoming events and limit meeting time to just what is needed to accomplish goals.

a mix of both delivery methods, continuous participation provides a community of practice the ability to create the relationships that help develop the sense of trust and identity that defines the community (Hildreth, Kimble, & Wright, 2000). When building a virtual community of practice for faculty teaching online, it is important to be respectful of the enormous time demands that faculty face everyday. Synchronous meetings should be limited to just the amount of time needed to accomplish the goal of the meeting. Additionally, providing faculty a schedule of upcoming events, discussions, and the like, will ensure timely participation and allow faculty to plan their own schedules in advance. If meeting in a virtual space faculty may need instructions for participating via the medium.

Chapter 5
Implement

Abstract In the ADDIE model, implementation is the actual launch and daily workings of interventions planned and produced through the design process. The implementation phase usually involves communicating plans to learners, planning the logistics of instruction, and preparing the support for learners, instructors and any other key personnel involved in the educational process (Larson and Lockee, Streamlined ID: A practical guide to instructional design, Routledge, New York, NY, 2014). Implementation tasks for building a community of practice include facilitation, trust building, member recruitment, and ongoing training. This chapter will explore the many tasks required for an effective launch and execution of a thriving community of practice.

Keywords ADDIE • Implementation • Facilitation • Trust building • Support • Mentoring • Community of practice • Virtual community of practice • Faculty development • Professional development • Domain • Community • Practice

5.1 Fundamental Element: Domain (Table 5.1)

5.1.1 Launch Community of Practice

When ready to implement a community of practice it is important to hold an event to introduce the community to the larger organization and potential members. Wenger, McDermott, and Snyder (2002) suggested that a visible launch with endorsement from management allows people to become more aware of the community, its focus, and potential benefits. When launching a virtual community of practice for faculty teaching at a distance, a face-to-face event may provide a way for relationships and trust to form for members. Hildreth, Kimble, and Wright (2000) conducted a study of two internationally distributed communities of practice and found that the community of practice that engaged in a face-to-face meeting

Table 5.1 Operationalization of domain related tasks during the implementation phase

Task	Faculty development operationalized example
Launch the community of practice (Wenger et al., 2002).	Launch community with a kick off event to showcase institutional support.
	Encourage a face-to-face event to build stronger relationships, richer interactions, and more knowledge sharing in the virtual community of practice.
Design opportunities interaction with outside expertise (Probst & Borzillo, 2008; Wenger et al., 2002).	Use synchronous communication tools to allow for guest speakers, colleagues from other universities, or other experts in the field to interact with community members.

formed more quickly and developed more meaningful interactions that led to richer knowledge sharing. Whether virtual or face-to-face or a combination of both, launching the community of practice with an event of some kind will likely attract broader support and participation (Wenger et al., 2002).

5.1.2   Include Outside Expertise

As discussed in earlier sections, providing opportunities for community of practice members to interact with outside expertise can mitigate problems arising from iso-lated communities of practice (Wenger et al., 2002). Probst and Borzillo (2008) found that organizations wishing to form and sustain communities of practice must design regular interactions with outside expertise. When implementing a virtual community of practice for faculty teaching at a distance, it is possible to design opportunities for faculty to interact with experts from other universities or from distance learning associations. With travel costs prohibiting many potential experts from traveling, using synchronous online tools to introduce.

5.2   Fundamental Element: Community (Table 5.2)

5.2.1   Build Trust

Ardichvili, Page, and Wentling (2002) noted that building trust is a critical compo-nent in the development of a community of practice and cited the lack of trust among members as one of the reasons that communities of practice fail. Trust build-ing must employ a comprehensive approach that examines both designed interac-tions and knowledge-sharing mechanisms. Both approaches are necessary for fostering trust in a community of practice (Jarvenpaa & Leidner, 1998; Wenger et al., 2002). No matter what the context of the community of practice, there must

Table 5.2 Operationalization of community related tasks during the implementation phase

Task	Faculty development operationalized example
Promote trust within the community membership (Hildreth et al., 2000; Probst & Borzillo, 2008; Wenger et al., 2002).	Engage in trust building activities including "hand holding" support and encourage participation with no judgment (core facilitators).
Mentor new members (Borzillo et al., 2011; Palloff & Pratt, 1999; Wenger et al., 2002).	Help new members navigate community of practice norms and expectations, improve instructional practices, and engage in scholarly work through mentoring program.
Facilitate discussions (Clawson & Bostrom, 1996; Fischer, 1998; Gray, 2004; Palloff & Pratt, 1999; Wenger et al., 2002).	Encourage instructional best practice knowledge sharing, thoughtful discussions, mediate discussion, provide answers to member questions, and provide technical support. Be aware of facilitator role dimensions and associated tasks (See Table 5.3).
Recruit new core leadership/facilitation group members (Gongla & Rizzuto, 2001; Wenger et al., 2002).	Plan for succession. Recruit new core members and leaders to replace outgoing leaders and to promote fresh ideas.

be significant effort to build trust among all participants (Wenger et al., 2002). If participants do not feel comfortable participating, they will not participate. During the earliest stages, the community of practice relies heavily on the core leadership to promote trust with and among participants. Wang and Chen (2009) discovered that higher-order collaborative problem solving was only possible when trust was fostered through social interactions and conversation. By studying the interactions of email, bulletin boards, and threaded discussions of online courses, Chih-Hsiung and McIsaac (2002) determined that incorporating concepts such as building trust online, providing "hand-holding" techniques, support, and promoting informal relationships can help make online learning environments more interactive and improve the sense of community (Chih-Hsiung & McIsaac, 2002). Core group members must be available to foster trust.

Virtual communities of practice must strive to create a base of trust among members by intentionally connecting people and finding multiple opportunities for members to interact and build relationships (Wenger et al., 2002). Much of the promotion of trust must be facilitated by the core membership or by the community facilitators (Gray, 2004; Palloff & Pratt, 1999). Jarvenpaa and Leidner (1998) researched trust in virtual teams and found that trust is developed in stages. According to the authors, in early stages trust is fostered when members are given opportunities for social exchanges or interactions, are allowed to suggest topics for discussion, and communication is enthusiastic and supportive. In later stages trust can be facilitated through regular intervals of interactions, substantive and prompt feedback, and rotating leadership roles (Jarvenpaa & Leidner, 1998).

When promoting trust in a virtual community of practice for faculty teaching online courses, core members or facilitators can deliberately plan and hold social events where members can interact with colleagues, interact regularly with members, be responsive to member's needs, and establish rules for knowledge sharing and conflict resolution. Core members or facilitators must be aware of the institutional culture and encourage an environment of reciprocity.

5.2.2 Mentor New Members

Once a community of practice is established and relationships have formed, new members will need to learn how to navigate the established norms and expectations of the community while overcoming social nuances. Mentoring new members is a key function of the community of practice core group. When researching how members of a community of practice move from periphery to active membership, Borzillo, Aznar, and Schmitt (2011) found that in the early stages of membership, community of practice leaders played a significant role in the movement. A formal mentorship program for new members can enhance the community by stabilizing membership, steering reification efforts, and enhancing the professional development for core membership (Wenger et al., 2002).

Participants in a typical community of practice serve in different roles and are participate in various ways. There are opportunities for all participants to find identity and to learn from a community of practice, even when participation is on the periphery (Brown, Collins, & Duguid, 1989). Wenger (1998) identified five trajectories or paths for participants to find identity in a community of practice: (a) peripheral trajectories—the outside edge of a community that provides participants access to a community, but never leads to full participation, (b) inbound trajectories—participants are invested in becoming active members of the community even though they may still be on the periphery of the community, (c) insider trajectories—full membership, but a commitment to continued improvement through new demands, (d) boundary trajectories—participants sustain an identity that spans and connects different communities of practice, and (e) outbound trajectories—participants no matter the cause are in the process of leaving the community and developing new identities.

University faculty are often already accustomed to the benefits that mentoring programs provide. In a study of a group of women scholars navigating the academic tenure process through peer mentorship, Driscoll, Parkes, Tilley-Lubbs, Brill, and Pitts Bannister (2009) reported that through collaboration and mentoring, individuals found independence and clear sense of direction for scholarship. Wildman, Hable, Preston, and Magliaro (2000) explored a faculty collaboration group at Virginia Tech and reported greater problem solving through a learning community. A formal mentoring program for new members of a community of practice for faculty teaching at a distance should provide guidance for navigating the community of practice and help faculty improve instructional practices while providing an avenue for scholarly research in the field.

5.2.3   Facilitation

Facilitation of any online learning community requires a strong presence by a group leader, facilitator, or instructor (Garrison, Anderson, & Archer, 1999). In order to maintain or sustain an active community of practice there must a concerted effort by facilitators to keep participants engaged through collaboration, problem solving, knowledge building and sharing, feedback, and providing opportunities for members to contribute to the larger organization by adding to the existing knowledge base (Gongla & Rizzuto, 2001; Wenger et al., 2002). Members of the core leadership group often serve in a facilitative role to guide discussions, find consensus for goals, and navigate the group through growth (Fischer, 1998; Palloff & Pratt, 1999; Wenger, 1998). Facilitators should lead meetings or events, form dialogue opportunities for community participants to engage in peer interactions, encourage knowledge construction, and mediate community coalescence (Bielaczyc & Collins, 1999; Wenger, 1998). There are many roles and tasks associated with facilitating discussion, meetings, and knowledge sharing in online environments. Clawson and Bostrom (1996) identified 16 different facilitator role dimensions that are essential for effective facilitation of interactions in computer-mediated environments (see Table 5.3).

Using the facilitator role dimensions and associated tasks as defined by Clawson and Bostrom (1996), it is possible to create clear expectations for community facilitators. At minimum, community facilitators should be aware of the many role dimensions and associated tasks. The role of group facilitators in a virtual community of practice for online teaching faculty will vary, but the focus of the facilitation should be to guide community members to share instructional best practices, mediate conflicts as they arise, promote rich discussions, answer questions, encourage networking, and provide technical support as needed.

5.2.4   Recruit New Core Group Members

As mentioned in earlier sections, building and maintaining a community of practice requires a strong group of core members and leaders. Over time, community of practice members cycle through the community and core members move on from the community or step into different roles within the community (Wenger, 1998). Planning for succession and finding new core members are important tasks for community leaders. It is possible to mitigate problems that may arise from a leadership vacuum caused when core members leave without defined successors. Leaders should plan for succession. Wenger et al. (2002) suggested rotating leadership roles through the core membership. A rotating membership can prepare members to take on new leadership roles as needed. Succession planning must address how to recruit new core member and leaders. Potential core members or leaders should be experts, thought leaders, practitioners, or midcareer professionals who might like or can be encouraged to take a more active role in the community of practice (Wenger et al., 2002). For more information about recruiting new members for a virtual community of practice refer to *Identify and Recruit Core Group* in the Analysis section.

Table 5.3 Facilitator role dimensions and associated tasks

Facilitator role dimension	Associated tasks
Plan and design the meeting	• Plan the meeting ahead of time. • Include meeting leaders/initiators in planning. • Develop clear meeting outcomes. • Design agenda and activities based on outcome, time frame, and group characteristics.
Listen to, clarify, and integrate information	• Really listen to what the group is saying and make an effort to make sense out of it. • Clarify goals, agenda, terms and definitions with group.
Demonstrate flexibility	• Adapt agenda or meeting activities on the spot as needed. • Can do more than one thing as a time.
Keep group outcome-focused	• Clearly communicate outcomes to the group upfront. • Make outcome visible to the group. • Keep group focused on and moving toward its outcome.
Create and reinforce an open, positive, and participative environment	• Draw out individuals by asking questions. • Use activities and technology to get people involved from the start. • Handle dominant people to ensure equal participation.
Select and prepare appropriate technology	• Match computer-based tools to the task(s) and outcome(s) the group wants to accomplish. • Select tools that fit group makeup.
Direct and manage the meetings	• Use the agenda to guide the group. • Use technology effectively to manage the group. • Set the stage for meeting and each activity. • Set time limits, enforces roles and ground rules.
Develops and asks the "right" questions	• Consider how to word and ask the "best" questions that encourage thought and participation.
Promote ownership and encourage group responsibility	• Help group take responsibility for and ownership of meeting outcomes and results. • Turn the floor over to others.
Actively build rapport and relationships	• Demonstrate responsiveness and respect for people, being sensitive to emotions. • Develop constructive relationships with and among members. • Greet and mingle with group.
Demonstrate self-awareness and self-expression	• Recognize and deal with own behavior and feelings. • Comfortable being self. • Keep personal ego out of the way of the group.
Manage conflict and negative emotions constructively	• Provide techniques to help group deal with conflict. • Gather and check group opinions and agreement level in disputes.
Encourage/support multiple perspectives	• Encourage looking at issues from different points of view. • Use techniques, metaphors, stories, and examples to get the group to consider different frames of reference.
Understand technology and its capabilities	• Know how to operate the system. • Clearly understand tools and their functions and capabilities. • Figure out and solves common technical difficulties.
Create comfort with and promote understanding of the technology and technology outputs.	• Introduce and explain technology to group. • Address negative comments and inconveniences caused by technology.
Present information to group	• Give clear and explicit instructions. • Use clear and concise language in presenting ideas. • Give group written information.

Note. From "Research-Driven Facilitation Training for Computer-Supported Environments," by V. K. Clawson and R. P. Bostrom, 1996, *Group Decision and Negotiation*, *5*, p. 7–29. 1996 Kluwer Academic Publishers. Adapted with permission

5.3 Fundamental Element: Practice (Table 5.4)

5.3.1 Provide Medium/Tool Training

In order for members to participate in knowledge sharing in the virtual environment they must first know how to navigate the medium and use the associated tools. Participants must feel comfortable with any tool used in the virtual environment or they will not participate (Sharratt & Usoro, 2003). Facilitators are responsible for technical support, technical knowledge, and for providing training for use in knowledge sharing tools (Chih-Hsiung & McIsaac, 2002; Gray, 2004). It is not necessary to hold a formal training on the use of the tool associated with the community of practice. Many online technologies have prepared tutorials or training materials that can provide necessary information for participants. If no tutorials or training materials are available, the creation of tutorials will provide participants with the help they need to successfully participate in community activities. As the community grows, making such materials available and accessible for members can minimize technical support issues and promote knowledge sharing (Wenger et al., 2002).

5.3.2 Build and Organize a Knowledge Repository

One of the main goals for a virtual community of practice is the development of a knowledge-sharing repository. Zhao and Bishop (2011) found that there must not only be a knowledge building component for an online community of practice, but also opportunities for interaction and meaning making as well. How a repository is organized will depend on the tools selected during the design phase. An institution supported learning management system (LMS) may have tools such as wikis or chats, but most have threaded discussion forums. Knowledge can be shared through

Table 5.4 Operationalization of practice related tasks during the implementation phase

Task	Faculty development operationalized example
Provide training for interaction and knowledge sharing through the virtual medium (Chih-Hsiung & McIsaac, 2002; Wenger et al., 2002).	Provide access to tutorials or other training materials for how to use the medium or tools to share knowledge and interact with other faculty participants.
Build and organize a knowledge repository (Scardamalia & Bereiter, 1994; Wenger et al., 2002; Zhao & Bishop, 2011).	Avoid information overload by providing an organized repository.
	Provide facilitation to ensure knowledge is organized appropriately for knowledge sharing and knowledge seeking members.
Expand knowledge sharing to knowledge creation with well-defined research agenda (Waddock & Walsh, 1999; Wenger et al., 2002).	Engage faculty in reification efforts that add to the literature in the field of distance learning teaching and learning best practices.
	Encourage conference attendance and publication of research.

discussion and other forms of interaction. As topics are discussed, how the content is organized will be an important consideration. Virtual community environments must be mindful of the knowledge overload that may happen when communicating or building knowledge in electronic environments (Hemp, 2009). As knowledge is shared or created in a virtual community of practice through threaded discussions, information can easily become overwhelming and disorganized. Hiltz and Turoff (1985) found that the design and structure of online discussion systems must include facilities for users to control and structure online discussions to ensure interactions did not lead to knowledge overload. Organizing the repository is critical to successful knowledge sharing.

Given that repositories have multiple modes for members to engage and interact with one another, there must be a deliberate design for how knowledge is shared in electronic environments (Scardamalia & Bereiter, 1994). Effective facilitation and planning can overcome problems associated with organizing a repository. Since knowledge repositories are meant to meet the needs of both knowledge sharers and knowledge seekers, community of practice facilitators should organize discussion threads by topic and moderate posts (Wenger et al., 2002). To minimize confusion, the repository should also delineate personal and public spaces. Predetermined criteria should describe where in the repository to hold informal discussion or chats, while reserving special spaces for more formal discussion and reification (Wenger et al., 2002).

5.3.3 Expand to Research Agenda

Reification is an important outcome for communities of practice. Without engaged knowledge creation a community of practice is relegated to a social group (Wenger, 1998; Wenger et al., 2002). In order to maintain membership and drive participation, communities of practice must also develop a plan for innovation or knowledge creation. West (2009) insists that communities of practice must do more than just provide members with competence or meaning making. Instead, communities of practice should become communities of innovation by shifting focus from just maintaining the status quo to creating and fostering an innovation (West, 2009). In their research on a university-wide community of practice, Waddock and Walsh (1999) found that engaging faculty and administrators in a variety of collaborative reification efforts including research, publications, grants, community outreach, and internal professional development efforts grew and sustained the community of practice. A community of practice for faculty interested in improving their online teaching practices can easily emulate the model as described by Waddock and Walsh (1999).

Chapter 6
Evaluation

Abstract In the ADDIE model, evaluation is an ongoing process. Evaluation ensures that the all components of design are addressing the gap or need, while providing for continuous improvement. Evaluating a community of practice requires a systematic plan that is specific to the community being evaluated. Evaluation must occur through all phases of community design from conception through implementation and continuously through maintenance (Schwier et al., Instructional designers' perceptions of their agency: Tales of change and community, In M. Keppell (Ed.), Instructional design: Case studies in communities of practice (pp. 1–18), Information Science Publishing, Hershey, PA, 2007). Designed communities often fail because they are not valued as contributors to the knowledge of the organization but rather as social gatherings or groups (Wenger, 2010). This chapter will explore how a community of practice for teaching faculty might be evaluated in the areas of domain, community, and practice.

Keywords ADDIE • Evaluation • Objectives • Evaluation plan • Kirkpatrick's Four Level Evaluation Model • Performance improvement • Community of practice • Virtual community of practice • Faculty development • Professional development • Domain • Community • Practice

6.1 Fundamental Element: Domain (Table 6.1)

6.1.1 Effectiveness of the Community in Context

A virtual community of practice for faculty teaching at a distance can prove its worth to the institution through systematic evaluation. Organizational leaders are often concerned with the bottom line and want to know that there is a return on investment (Wenger, McDermott, & Snyder, 2002). Evaluating whether the community of practice is providing value to the organization and is in alignment with

M.A. Bond and B.B. Lockee, *Building Virtual Communities of Practice*   39
for Distance Educators, SpringerBriefs in Educational Communications and Technology,
DOI 10.1007/978-3-319-03626-7_6, © Springer International Publishing Switzerland 2014

Table 6.1 Operationalization of domain-related tasks during the evaluation phase

Task	Faculty development operationalized example
Evaluate the effectiveness of the community in context within the larger organization (Probst & Borzillo, 2008; Wenger et al., 2002).	Use evaluations that show value to the larger institution and alignment with institutional goals. Incorporate Kirkpatrick's Evaluation Model for a comprehensive approach. Evaluate sparingly so as not to over burden the faculty participants.

the organizational goals is key to sustaining a community of practice. If a community of practice loses institutional support or is perceived to lack value, it will lose validity and participation (Wenger et al., 2002). Institutional goals are generally wrapped around the improvement of instructional practices, student engagement, and other student-centered areas. Ways to implement evaluative processes that show alignment will vary from institution but might include: student end-of-course surveys, faculty climate surveys, or volume of distance-learning related research. Other evaluations as described in later fundamental element sections can also be used to show alignment with institutional goals.

A comprehensive evaluation can determine whether the community of practice is meeting institutional and faculty needs. When conducting the gap analysis it is possible to create a plan for evaluation that measures whether the gap has been mitigated and if the community of practice is creating value for the institution and faculty (Wenger, Trayner, & de Laat, 2011). Core members or community facilitators should work together to determine a regular schedule for evaluation and administer evaluations accordingly. It is possible to use Kirkpatrick's Four-Level Evaluation Model to evaluate the virtual community of practice for faculty teaching online (Wenger et al., 2011). Kirkpatrick's Four Level Evaluation Model asserts that professional development should be evaluated with four possible outcomes in mind:

- Reactions—did participants enjoy the experience?
- Learning—have participants increased knowledge?
- Behavior—has knowledge led to new behaviors?
- Results—has there been an organizational benefit?

Building on Kirkpatrick's model, Table 6.2 details the evaluation focus for each level and presents corresponding questions for a virtual community of practice for faculty teaching at a distance.

6.2   Fundamental Element: Community (Table 6.3)

6.2.1   Level of Trust and Quality/Quantity of Interactions

Evaluation of a community of practice can be conducted by analyzing the level of trust displayed in the online interactions. If trust is not built in a community of practice it will show through the quality and quantity of interactions in the online forum

Table 6.2 Virtual community of practice evaluation based on Kirkpatrick's Four-Level Model

Level and technique (Kirkpatrick, 1998)	Possible questions/areas for evaluation
Level 1-Reaction (Faculty perceptions of the community of practice) Surveys for participant perceptions.	• Are you satisfied with the community of practice? • Is it easy to use? • What do you like/dislike about the community? • Are the facilitators friendly?
Level 2-Learning (The extent to which faculty participants change attitudes, improve knowledge, and/or increase skill as a result of participating in the community of practice) Survey for perceptions, evaluate for learning through discourse analysis.	• What skills, knowledge, attitude has changed as a result of your participation? • Can you describe how you will incorporate what you have learned in your courses? • Is there quality knowledge being shared by members?
Level 3-Behavior (Extent that faculty are using the newly acquired skill, knowledge, or attitude in their online teaching) End of Course Evaluations, Peer Evaluations	• Comparison of end of course evaluations • Faculty peer review for online course development and teaching.
Level 4-Results (The extent of the return on investment or value to the institution that the community provides) Institutional measures	• Increase in online courses being developed or taught? • Decreased attrition in online courses? • Increased enrollments in online courses?

Table 6.3 Operationalization of community-related tasks during the evaluation phase

Task	Faculty development operationalized example
Evaluate active membership through quality and quantity of member interactions and level of trust (Alem & Kravis, 2005; Wenger et al., 2011).	Use existing artifacts (forum discussions, wiki posts, research efforts, etc.) to measure trust and participation by analyzing the quantity and quality of member interactions.
Evaluate participant perceptions of learning and performance improvement (Verburg & Andriessen, 2006; Wenger et al., 2011).	Use predetermined criteria to gather member perceptions of value, learning, or performance improvement.

(Palloff & Pratt, 1999). Wenger et al. (2011) identified five ways to measure quantity of interactions: (a) attendance at meetings, (b) number and characteristics of active participants, (c) subscribers, (d) logs and website statistics, and (e) participant lists from synchronous meetings. Alem and Kravis (2005) evaluated the success of a virtual community of practice based on active membership, lurkers, number of messages per participant, on topic discussions, level of trust and satisfaction, and average length of membership. This information can be easily gathered by conducting an analysis of the artifacts, discussion threads, and other documentation developed by the community of practice. Community of practice leaders can learn a great deal about the health of a community of practice by evaluating the quality and quantity of interactions (Ke & Hoadley, 2009; Wenger et al., 2002).

6.2.2 Perceptions of Learning and Improved Performance

Member perceptions of a community of practice can be used as an evaluative tool. Verburg and Adriessen (2006) used community of practice member perceptions to evaluate the effectiveness of seven communities of practice. Wenger et al. (2011) argued that the value of a community of practice can be measured by collecting participant perceptions of learning or improved performance. Though participant perceptions of learning or improvement does not always translate into real learning or improvement, it can help give a view into how participants perceive the value of the community of practice. Wenger et al. (2011) constructed an evaluative tool with a variety of questions covering five major value domains (see Appendix B). The instrument is designed to capture community of practice member perceptions of the value created from participation in a community of practice.

While the potential evaluation questions in Appendix B are extensive, it is not necessary to use all of the questions to conduct an evaluation of members. Several questions from each value domain can provide a picture of member perceptions of the value created from a community of practice.

6.3 Fundamental Element: Practice (Table 6.4)

6.3.1 Effectiveness of Medium

In order to ensure that all components of a community of practice are examined for effectiveness, evaluations should also focus on the technology employed to host a virtual community of practice. Teo, Chan, Wei, and Zhang (2003) suggested evaluating the usefulness and usability of the medium housing the community of practice. Additionally, researchers in the same study examined perceived usefulness, sense of belonging, perceived ease of use, intentions for use, and adaptivity to evaluate the effectiveness of the medium for a virtual community of practice (Teo et al., 2003). Getting feedback on the medium from community of practice members can help core members make decisions about adjustments to the medium or whether to change the medium altogether.

Table 6.4 Operationalization of practice related tasks during the evaluation phase

Task	Faculty development operationalized example
Evaluate the effectiveness of the knowledge sharing medium (Teo et al., 2003).	Evaluate for perceived usability, perceived usefulness, sense of belonging, and adaptivity.
Evaluate quality and quantity of knowledge sharing (Derry & DuRussel, 1999; Wenger et al., 2011).	Use existing artifacts in the knowledge repository to analyze quality and quantity of knowledge sharing. Include any past or ongoing research projects.

6.3.2 Quality/Quantity of Knowledge Sharing

A community of practice can be evaluated by analyzing the quality and quantity of knowledge that is created (Derry & DuRussel, 1999). Wenger et al. (2002) suggested that the knowledge repository that is created at the center of the community is itself a tool for evaluation. A thriving community should have a robust knowledge repository of shared knowledge and co-constructed new knowledge to analyze. A community that is fading or stuck in a rut will have little or no knowledge repository. When analyzing a knowledge repository, evaluators should look for intensity of discussions, challenges of assumptions, length of threads, the sharing of experiences of practice into the space, debates on important issues, feedback on quality of responses to queries, new knowledge construction, and any reification efforts (Wenger et al., 2011). Evaluation of the quality and quantity of knowledge sharing in a virtual community of practice for faculty teaching at a distance should include an analysis of existing artifacts, discussions, and any research projects associated with improving online teaching and learning practices. Table 6.2 provides guidance for conducting practice-related evaluations.

6.4 Caveat

A critical component of instructional design is evaluation. Evaluating a community of practice requires a systematic plan for assessment that is specific to the community being evaluated. Evaluation must occur through all phases of community design from conception through implementation and continuously through maintenance (Schwier, Campbell, & Kenny, 2007). Discretion must be used when evaluating a virtual community of practice for faculty teaching at a distance (Schroeder, 2011). Faculty members have many commitments and may become annoyed if the community of practice is constantly being evaluated. Communities of practice have a tendency to fall apart when members feel that there is an effort to institutionalize the community of practice (Dubé, Bourhis, & Jacob, 2006). Evaluation of the community of practice should be done sparingly. Evaluation can include all elements in one evaluation or concentrate on perceived areas of weakness (Wenger et al., 2011). It is important to apply caution and institutional considerations when undertaking any task as defined in the guidelines.

Chapter 7
Conclusion and Next Steps

Keywords ADDIE • Community of practice • Virtual community of practice • Faculty development • Professional development • Online learning • Online teaching

Though more institutions report an increase in online programs and course offerings, faculty report poor institutional support for teaching faculty engaged in online courses (Sloan National Commission on Online Learning, 2013). With the growing number of faculty engaged in online teaching and learning there is a need for innovative approaches to faculty professional development and support (Association of Public and Land-grant Universities-Sloan National Commission on Online Learning, 2009). Communities of practice for faculty teaching at a distance may provide opportunities for professional development and support. Guidelines for designing a virtual community of practice demonstrate how research-based tasks may be mapped to the design tasks in the ADDIE model.

Though this set of guidelines are designed to support faculty engaged in distance learning, instructional designers, faculty support personnel, and/or faculty developers may also be able to use the guidelines that emerged from this study to design virtual communities of practice for all university teaching faculty. The guidelines are meant to solve certain support or development-related issues affecting faculty. There will likely be instances, situations, or institutions where these guidelines for building a community of practice for faculty teaching at a distance may not be as appropriate. Additionally, the guidelines are not meant to be linear and should be employed in a rather cyclical manner. For instance, if a virtual community of practice already exists, there may not be a need for an intensive recruitment process. Instructional designers, support personnel, developers, and administrators can adapt the guidelines to meet their faculty or institutional needs.

7.1 Next Steps

Implementation of the guidelines is the appropriate next step in the development process of this framework. Given that design and development research is a continuous process of implementation and evaluation, the next phase of this study should test the guidelines in the field to explore how best to implement them, determine their feasibility, and identify any potential issues (Jonassen, Cernusca, & Ionas, 2007). Additional research and testing of these guidelines may also contribute to the instructional design, faculty development, and community of practice literature.

Appendix A: Analysis Phase Sample Community Design Planning Document

Use this document to perform relevant tasks for building a community of practice for faculty teaching at a distance.

Intent of the community of practice for faculty teaching at a distance:

_____

_____

Topics/Main ideas connecting potential faculty community members:

_____

_____

How does the community of practice for faculty teaching at a distance align with the larger university, department, or college?

_____

_____

Is there organizational support? Explain.

_____

_____

M.A. Bond and B.B. Lockee, *Building Virtual Communities of Practice for Distance Educators*, SpringerBriefs in Educational Communications and Technology, DOI 10.1007/978-3-319-03626-7, © Springer International Publishing Switzerland 2014

If not, how will organizational support be secured?

_____

_____

Who are potential thought leaders, facilitators, or core members?

_____

_____

How will potential core members be recruited? Remember to incorporate factors that motivate faculty to participate.

_____

_____

Who are the potential community of practice faculty members?

_____

_____

Will a community of practice meet the needs of potential faculty members? Explain how.

_____

_____

How will potential faculty members be recruited?

_____

_____

What are common knowledge sharing needs of the potential faculty members?

_____

_____

Appendix B: Questions for Evaluating of Community of Practice Member Perceptions

Perceived values (Wenger, Trayner, & de Laat, 2011)	Questions
Immediate value: What was my experience of it?	• How much participation was there?
	• What was the quality of the mutual engagement?
	• Was it fun, inspiring, convivial?
	• How relevant to me was the activity/interaction?
	• With whom did I interact or make connections?
	• Which connections are most influential on my own development?
Potential value: What has all this activity produced?	• How has my participation changed me?
	• Have I acquired new skills or knowledge?
	• Has my understanding of the domain or my perspective changed?
	• Do I feel more inspired by the work I do?
	• Have I gained confidence in my ability to engage in practice?
	• How has my participation changed my social relationships?
	• What access to new people have I gained?
	• Do I know them well enough to know what they can contribute to my learning?
	• Do I trust them enough to turn to them for help?
	• Do I feel less isolated?
	• Am I gaining a positive reputation from my participation?
	• What access to resources has my participation given me?
	• Do I have new tools, methods, or processes?
	• Do I have access to documents or sources of information I would not have otherwise?
	• What position has the community acquired?
	• Has the community changed the recognition of our expertise?
	• Have we acquired a new voice through our collective learning?
	• How has my participation transformed my view of learning?
	• Do I see opportunities for learning that I did not see before?
	• Do I now see opportunities for convening a community of practice or network in the service of learning that I did not see before?

(continued)

M.A. Bond and B.B. Lockee, *Building Virtual Communities of Practice for Distance Educators*, SpringerBriefs in Educational Communications and Technology, DOI 10.1007/978-3-319-03626-7, © Springer International Publishing Switzerland 2014

(continued)

Perceived values (Wenger, Trayner, & de Laat, 2011)	Questions
Applied value: What difference has it made to my practice/life/context?	• Where have I used the products of the community/network? • Where did I apply a skill I acquired? • When did I leverage a community/network connection in the accomplishment of a task? • Was I able to enlist others in pursuing a cause I care about? • When and how did I use a document or tool that the community produced or made accessible? • How was an idea or suggestion implemented? At what level—individual, team/unit, organization
Realized value: What difference has it made to my ability to achieve what matters to me or other stakeholders?	• What aspects of my performance has my participation in community/network affected? • Did I save time or achieve something new? • Am I more successful generally? How? • What effect did the implementation of an idea have? • Did any of this affect some metrics that are used to evaluate performance? • What has my organization been able to achieve because of my participation in community/network?
Reframing value: Has it changed my or other stakeholders' understandings and definitions of what matters?	• Has the process of social learning led to a reflection on what matters? • Has this changed someone's understanding of what matters? • Does this suggest new criteria and new metrics to include in evaluation? • How has this new understanding affected those who have the power to define criteria of success? • Has this new understanding translated into institutional changes? • Has a new framework or system evolved or been created as a result of this new understanding?

References

Alem, L., & Kravis, S. (2005). Design and evaluation of an online learning community: A case study at *CSIRO. SIGGROUP Bulletin, 25*(1), 20–24. doi:http://doi.acm.org/10.1145/1067699.1067703

American Productivity & Quality Center. (2001). *Building and sustaining communities of practice: Continuing success in knowledge management.* Houston, TX: American Productivity & Quality Center.

Ardichvili, A., Page, V., & Wentling, T. (2002). Virtual knowledge-sharing communities of practice at caterpillar: Success factors and barriers. *Performance Improvement Quarterly, 15*(3), 94–113. doi:10.1111/j.19378327.2002.tb00258.x.

Association of Public and Land-grant Universities-Sloan National Commission on Online Learning. (2009). *Online learning as a strategic asset.* Retrieved November 4, 2009, from http://www.sloan-c.org/APLU_Reports

Bielaczyc, K., & Collins, A. (1999). Learning communities in classrooms: A reconceptualization of educational practice. In C. Reigeluth (Ed.), *Instructional design theories and models. A new paradigm of instructional theory* (Vol. 2, pp. 269–292). Mahwah, NJ: Lawrence Erlbaum Associates.

Bonk, C. J., & Dennen, V. P. (2003). Frameworks for research, design, benchmarks, training, and pedagogy in web-based distance education. In M. G. Moore & W. G. Anderson (Eds.), *Handbook of distance education* (pp. 331–349). Mahwah, NJ: Lawrence Erlbaum Associates.

Borzillo, S., Aznar, S., & Schmitt, A. (2011). A journey through communities of practice: How and why members move from the periphery to the core. *European Management Journal, 29*(1), 25–42. doi:10.1016/j.emj.2010.08.004.

Brown, J. S., Collins, A., & Duguid, P. (1989). Situated cognition and the culture of learning. *Educational Researcher, 18*(1), 32–42.

Carroll, J., Choo, C., Dunlap, D., Isenhour, P., Kerr, S., MacLean, A., et al. (2003). Knowledge management support for teachers. *Educational Technology Research and Development, 51*(4), 42–64.

Cennamo, K., & Kalk, D. (2005). *Real world instructional design.* Toronto, ON: Thomson Learning.

Chih-Hsiung, T., & McIsaac, M. (2002). The relationship of social presence and interaction in online classes. *American Journal of Distance Education, 16*(3), 131.

Clawson, V., & Bostrom, R. (1996). Research-driven facilitation training for computer supported environments. *Group Decision and Negotiation, 5*(1), 7–29. doi:10.1007/BF02404174.

Cox, G., Carr, T., & Hall, M. (2004). Evaluating the use of synchronous communication in two blended courses. *Journal of Computer Assisted Learning, 20*(3), 183–193.

Derry, S. J., & DuRussel, L. A. (1999, July). *Assessing knowledge construction in online learning communities.* Paper presented at the Annual Meeting of the International Society for Artificial Intelligence in Education, Lemans, France (ERIC Document Reproduction No. Ed 446897).

M.A. Bond and B.B. Lockee, *Building Virtual Communities of Practice for Distance Educators*, SpringerBriefs in Educational Communications and Technology, DOI 10.1007/978-3-319-03626-7, © Springer International Publishing Switzerland 2014

Driscoll, L., Parkes, K. A., Tilley-Lubbs, G. A., Brill, J. M., & Pitts Bannister, V. R. (2009). Navigating the lonely sea: Peer mentoring and collaboration among aspiring women scholars. *Mentoring&TutoringforPartnershipinLearning,17*(1),5–21.doi:10.1080/13611260802699532.

Dubé, L., Bourhis, A., & Jacob, R. (2006). Towards a typology of virtual communities of practice. *Interdisciplinary Journal of Information Knowledge and Management, 1*(1), 69–93.

Durkee, D., Brant, S., Nevin, P., Odell, A., Williams, G., Melomey, D., et al. (2009). Implementing e-learning and Web 2.0 innovation: Didactical scenarios and practical implications. *Industry and Higher Education, 23*(4), 293–300. doi:http://dx.doi.org/10.5367/000000009789346176

Fallah, N. (2011). Distributed form of leadership in communities of practice (CoPs). *International Journal of Emerging Sciences, 1*(3), 357–370.

Fischer, M. (1998). Using Lotus notes learning space for staff development in public schools. *Journal of Interactive Learning Research, 9*(3–4), 221–234.

Franklin, M. (2006). *Performance gap analysis: Tips, tools, and intelligence for trainers.* Alexandria, VA: ASTD Press.

Garrison, D. R., Anderson, T., & Archer, W. (1999). Critical inquiry in a text-based environment: Computer conferencing in higher education. *The Internet and Higher Education, 2*(2–3), 87–105. doi:10.1016/S1096-7516(00)00016-6.

Gongla, P., & Rizzuto, C. R. (2001). Evolving communities of practice: IBM Global Services experience. *IBM Systems Journal, 40*(4), 842–862. doi:10.1147/sj.404.0842.

Gongla, P., & Rizzuto, C. R. (2004). Where did that community go? Communities of practice that disappear. In P. Hildreth & C. Kimble (Eds.), *Knowledge networks: Innovation through communities of practice* (pp. 295–307). Hershey, PA: Idea Group.

Gray, P. H. (2001). The impact of knowledge repositories on power and control in the workplace. *Information Technology & People, 14*(4), 368–384.

Gray, B. (2004). Informal learning in an online community of practice. *Journal of Distance Education, 19*(1), 20–35.

Gustafson, K. L., & Branch, R. M. (2002). What is instructional design? In R. A. Reiser & J. V. Dempsey (Eds.), *Trends and issues in instructional design and technology* (pp. 16–25). Columbus, OH: Merrill Prentice Hall.

Heath, S., & McDonald, J. (2012). Creating community: One institution's experience with communities of practice. *Collected Essays on Learning and Teaching, 5*, 22–26.

Hemp, P. (2009). Death by information overload. *Harvard Business Review, 87*(9), 83–89.

Henning, P. H. (2004). Everyday cognition and situated learning. In D. Jonassen (Ed.), *Handbook of research on educational communications and technology* (pp. 143–168). Mahwah, NJ: Lawrence Erlbaum Associates.

Hildreth, P., Kimble, C., & Wright, P. (2000). Communities of practice in the distributed international environment. *Journal of Knowledge Management, 4*(1), 27–38.

Hiltz, S. R., & Turoff, M. (1985). Structuring computer-mediated communication systems to avoid information overload. *Communication of the ACM, 28*(7), 680–689.

Janis, I. L. (1972). *Victims of groupthink: A psychological study of foreign-policy decisions and fiascoes.* Boston, MA: Houghton Mifflin.

Jarvenpaa, S. L., & Leidner, D. E. (1998). Communication and trust in global virtual teams. *Journal of Computer-Mediated Communication, 3*(4), 1–36. doi:10.1111/j.1083-6101.1998.tb00080.x.

Jonassen, D., Cernusca, D., & Ionas, G. (2007). Constructivism and instructional design: The emergence of the learning sciences and design research. In R. A. Reiser & J. V. Dempsey (Eds.), *Trends and issues in instructional design and technology* (2nd ed., pp. 45–52). Upper Saddle River, NJ: Pearson.

Ke, F., & Hoadley, C. (2009). Evaluating online learning communities. *Educational Technology Research & Development, 57*(4), 487–510.

Kear, K. L. (2011). *Online and social networking communities: A best practice guide for educators.* New York, NY: Routledge.

Kirkpatrick, D. L. (1998). *Evaluating training programs: The four levels.* San Francisco, CA: Berrett-Koehler. Retrieved from http://ezproxy.lib.vt.edu:8080/login?url=http://search.ebscohost.com/login.aspx?direct=true&db=nlebk&AN=41336&scope=site.

Kiziltepe, Z. (2008). Motivation and demotivation of university teachers. *Teachers and Teaching, 14*(5–6), 515–530. doi:10.1080/13540600802571361.

Larson, M. B., & Lockee, B. B. (2014). *Streamlined ID: A practical guide to instructional design.* New York, NY: Routledge.

Lave, J., & Wenger, E. (1991). *Situated learning: Legitimate peripheral participation.* New York, NY: Cambridge University Press.

Lindkvist, L. (2005). Knowledge communities and knowledge collectivities: A typology of knowledge work in groups. *Journal of Management Studies, 42*(6), 1189–1210. doi:10.1111/j.1467-6486.2005.00538.x.

Mager, R. F. (1997). *Preparing instructional objectives: A critical tool in the development of effective instruction.* Atlanta, GA: CEP Press.

McDermott, R. (2001). *Knowing in community: 10 critical success factors in building communities of practice.* Retrieved from http://www.co-i-l.com/coil/knowledge-garden/cop/knowing.shtml

McLoughlin, C. (2001). Inclusivity and alignment: Principles of pedagogy, task and assessment design for effective cross-cultural online learning. *Distance Education, 22*(1), 7–29.

Meyer, L. H., & Evans, I. M. (2003). Motivating the professoriate: Why sticks and carrots are only for donkeys. *Higher Education Management and Policy, 15*, 151–168.

Morrison, G. R., Ross, S. M., Kemp, J. E., & Kalman, H. (2010). *Designing effective instruction.* Hoboken, NJ: John Wiley & Sons.

Ni, X., & Branch, R. M. (2010). Augmenting the ADDIE paradigm for instructional design. *Educational Technology, 48*(6), 16–19.

Ozdilek, Z., & Robeck, E. (2009). Operational priorities of instructional designers analyzed within the steps of the Addie instructional design model. *World Conference on Educational Sciences, Nicosia, North Cyprus, 4–7 February 2009, New Trends and Issues in Educational Sciences, 1*(1), 2046–2050. doi:10.1016/j.sbspro.2009.01.359.

Palloff, R., & Pratt, K. (1999). *Building learning communities in cyberspace: Effective strategies for the online classroom.* San Francisco, CA: Jossey-Bass.

Probst, G., & Borzillo, S. (2008). Why communities of practice succeed and why they fail. *European Management Journal, 26*(5), 335–347. doi:10.1016/j.emj.2008.05.003.

Richey, R. C., & Klein, J. D. (2007). *Design and development research: Methods, strategies and issues.* New York, NY: Routledge.

Richey, R. C., Klein, J. D., & Tracey, M. W. (2011). *The instructional design knowledge base: Theory, research, and practice.* New York, NY: Routledge.

Rogers, C. R., & Skinner, B. F. (1956). Some issues concerning the control of human behavior. *Science, 124*(3231), 1057–1066.

Scardamalia, M., & Bereiter, C. (1994). Computer support for knowledge-building communities. *The Journal of the Learning Sciences, 3*(3), 265–283.

Schroeder, C. M. (2011). *Coming in from the margin: Faculty development's emerging organizational development role in institutional change.* Sterling, VA: Stylus Publishing.

Schwier, R. A., Campbell, K., & Kenny, R. F. (2007). Instructional designers' perceptions of their agency: Tales of change and community. In M. Keppell (Ed.), *Instructional design: Case studies in communities of practice* (pp. 1–18). Hershey, PA: Information Science Publishing. doi:10.4018/978-1-59904322-7.ch001.

Sharratt, M., & Usoro, A. (2003). Understanding knowledge-sharing in online communities of practice. *Electronic Journal of Knowledge Management, 1*(2), 187.

Sherer, P. D., Shea, T. P., & Kristensen, E. (2003). Online communities of practice: A catalyst for faculty development. *Innovative Higher Education, 27*(3), 183.

Skinner, B. F. (1967). *Science and human behavior.* New York, NY: Free Press.

Sloan National Commission on Online Learning. (2013). *Changing course: Ten years of tracking online education in the United States.* Babson Park, MA: Babson Survey Research Group.

Smith, P. L., & Ragan, T. J. (2005). *Instructional design.* Hoboken, NJ: John Wiley & Sons.

Tarmizi, H., & de Vreede, G.-J. (2005). *A facilitation task taxonomy for a COP.* Proceedings of the Eleventh Americas Conference on Information Systems, Omaha, NE, USA, August 11th–14th 2005.

Teo, H.-H., Chan, H.-C., Wei, K.-K., & Zhang, Z. (2003). Evaluating information accessibility and community adaptivity features for sustaining virtual learning communities. *International Journal of Human-Computer Studies, 59*(5), 671–697. doi:10.1016/S10715819(03)00087-9.

Verburg, R. M., & Andriessen, J. H. (2006). The assessment of communities of practice. *Knowledge and Process Management, 13*(1), 13–25. doi:10.1002/kpm.2413.

Waddock, S., & Walsh, M. (1999). Paradigm shift: Toward a community-university community of practice. *International Journal of Organizational Analysis, 7*(3), 244–265.

Wang, Y., & Chen, N.-S. (2009). Criteria for evaluating synchronous learning Management systems: Arguments from the distance language classroom. *Computer Assisted Language Learning, 22*(1), 1–18. doi:10.1080/09588220802613773.

Wang, C.-C., & Lai, C.-Y. (2006). Knowledge contribution in the online virtual community: Capability and motivation. In J. Lang, F. Lin, & J. Wang (Eds.), *Knowledge science, engineering and management, lecture notes in computer science* (Vol. 4092, pp. 442–453). Berlin, Germany: Springer. Retrieved from http://dx.doi.org/10.1007/11811220_37

Wasko, M. M., & Faraj, S. (2005). Why should I share? Examining social capital and knowledge contribution in electronic networks of practice. *MIS Quarterly, 29*(1), 35–57.

Wenger, E. (1998). *Communities of practice: Learning, meaning, and identity*. New York, NY: Cambridge University Press.

Wenger, E. (2010). Communities of practice and social learning systems: The career of a concept. In C. Blackmore (Ed.), *Social learning systems and communities of practice* (pp. 179–198). Berlin: Springer Verlag and the Open University.

Wenger, E., McDermott, R. A., & Snyder, W. (2002). *Cultivating communities of practice a guide to managing knowledge*. Boston, MA: Harvard Business School Press.

Wenger, E., Trayner, B., & de Laat, M. (2011). *Promoting and assessing value creation in communities and networks: A conceptual framework*. The Netherlands: Ruud de Moor Centrum of The Open University.

West, R. (2009). What is shared? A framework for understanding shared innovation within communities. *Educational Technology Research and Development, 57*(3), 315–332.

Wildman, T., Hable, M., Preston, M., & Magliaro, S. (2000). Faculty student groups: Solving "good problems" through study, reflection, and collaboration. *Innovative Higher Education, 24*, 247–263.

Zhao, X., & Bishop, M. J. (2011). Understanding and supporting online communities of practice: Lessons learned from Wikipedia. *Educational Technology Research and Development, 59*(5), 711–735. doi:10.1007/s11423-011-9204-7.

Index

A
ADDIE model, 2–5, 45
  analysis
    community design planning document,
      14–15, 47–48
    community intent, determination of,
      9–10
    gap analysis, 8–9
    identify and recruit core group, 12–13
    knowledge sharing, infrastructure
      needs for, 14
    organizational alignment and support,
      assessment of, 11
    potential members, needs analysis, 13
    project scope, 10
  design
    core group, formation of, 21
    evaluation plan, 19–20
    instructional objectives, 17
    knowledge sharing and expectation
      design, 18–19
    media selection, 21, 22
    organizational goals/objectives,
      formation of, 17–19
  development
    core membership training, 27, 28
    designing interactions, 28–29
    membership recruitment, marketing
      strategies, 26–27
    onboarding new members, mechanisms
      for, 28
    problem mitigation, interventions to,
      23–25
    rewards/incentives plan, creation of,
      25–27
  evaluation

    community in context, effectiveness of,
      39–41
    interactions, quality/quantity of, 40–41
    knowledge sharing, quality/quantity
      of, 43
    medium, effectiveness of, 42
    perceptions of learning, 42, 49–50
    performance improvement, 42
    trust level, analysis of, 40
  guidelines, 2
  implementation
    core group members, recruitment of, 35
    facilitation, 35, 36
    knowledge-sharing repository,
      development of, 37–38
    launch community of practice, 31–32
    new members, mentoring program
      for, 34
    outside expertise, interaction with, 32
    research agenda, expand to, 38
    trust building, 32–34
    virtual medium/tool training, 37
  as project management tool, 2
Amnesia, 24, 25
Analysis
  community related tasks
    identify and recruit core group, 12–13
    potential members, needs analysis, 13
  domain-related tasks
    community intent, determination of,
      9–10
    gap analysis, 8–9
    organizational alignment and support,
      assessment of, 11
    project scope, 10
  practice related tasks

Made in the USA
Middletown, DE
10 November 2015